PRAISE FOR *WHAT'S MY AURA?*

"Not only did Mystic Michaela make a tricky topic incredibly easy to understand—the quiz also makes it possible for anyone to discover what their aura is. This has helped in everything from relationships to my career. *What's My Aura?* is a must-read!"

—RACHEL KHONA, writer featured in *Marie Claire*, *Allure*, and *Cosmopolitan*

"Mystic Michaela writes so clearly and compassionately about finding yourself through aura colors. On top of that, this book is a ton of fun. I'm going to get it for all my girlfriends!"

—ALLIE JONES, writer for *Gawker*

"Mystic Michaela's many insights are so spot-on and incredibly enlightening. My favorite thing about her (and her new book!) is her knack for explaining all things spiritual and mystical in a grounded, tangible, and easy-to-understand way, making the wisdom actionable and actually helpful in creating our best lives. She's guiding you back to your true self, which is the greatest gift of all."

—JESSICA ESTRADA, writer featured in *Well+Good* and *Refinery29*

WHAT'S MY

aura?

Learn Your Color, What It Means, and How You Can Embrace Your Unique Energy Signature

MYSTIC MICHAELA

Author of *The Angel Numbers Book*

ADAMS MEDIA

NEW YORK LONDON TORONTO SYDNEY NEW DELHI

dedication

To Scotty.

Adams Media
An Imprint of Simon & Schuster, Inc.
100 Technology Center Drive
Stoughton, Massachusetts 02072

First Adams Media hardcover edition December 2023

ADAMS MEDIA and colophon are registered trademarks of Simon & Schuster, Inc.

For information about special discounts for bulk purchases, please contact Simon & Schuster Special Sales at 1-866-506-1949 or business@simonandschuster.com.

The Simon & Schuster Speakers Bureau can bring authors to your live event. For more information or to book an event, contact the Simon & Schuster Speakers Bureau at 1-866-248-3049 or visit our website at www.simonspeakers.com.

Interior design by Kellie Emery
Images © 123RF/Christina Vartanova, Oksana Stepanenko

Manufactured in China

10 9 8 7 6 5 4 3 2 1

Library of Congress Cataloging-in-Publication Data
Names: Mystic Michaela, author.
Title: What's my aura? / Mystic Michaela, author of The angel numbers book.
Description: First Adams Media hardcover edition. | Stoughton, Massachusetts: Adams Media, 2023. | Includes index.
Identifiers: LCCN 2023008111 | ISBN 9781507221310 (hc) | ISBN 9781507221358 (ebook)
Subjects: LCSH: Aura.
Classification: LCC BF1389.A8 M97 2023 | DDC 133.8/92--dc23/eng/20230504
LC record available at https://lccn.loc.gov/2023008111

ISBN 978-1-5072-2131-0
ISBN 978-1-5072-2135-8 (ebook)

contents

author's note

Seeing colors around people for my entire life was confusing to me. I thought everyone saw these individualized hues around the people they met. For a long time, it didn't occur to me that others couldn't see them. Without knowing what they meant, I had to make my own interpretations through my experiences.

I would see colorful hues around people and could understand when what they said didn't align with the vibration they emitted. Some auras looked better than others. They had healthier glows and clearer colors. I saw that those people lived a bit differently than most: They lived to serve a purpose that made sense to themselves instead of focusing on what the world thought they should do or be.

Still, it wasn't until I was teaching middle school students that I realized auras were brilliant beacons of insight, which led me to uncover the students' authentic selves. Using the aura colors I saw, I would differentiate instruction based on students' individual needs. I noticed that certain auras required different exercises to make sense of the curriculum, and I realized that my students could better understand the way I spoke if I customized my delivery to their aura.

The energetic signatures around all of us are unique; no two are alike. Even though many people may not see them, the frequencies these signatures emit can be felt by everyone and everything. By reading and using this book, I hope that *you* will find your authentic self where it has always been: right inside of you. My wish for you is to uncover your true self and feel its power—and when you do, to use that power to live the purposeful life you are worthy of living.

introduction

Have you ever felt unsure of what decision to make in your career, romance, or another part of life? Maybe you've been stuck between two choices, afraid to make the "wrong" move forward. Or perhaps you're confused about what you truly want versus what others suggest is right for you. There is a force around you that holds your soul's plan—a unique and colorful energetic signature that can guide you in making these choices and more. This is your aura. And understanding this energetic signature allows you to control your present and future in the most authentic way possible.

In *What's My Aura?*, you will begin the journey of understanding not only what your aura colors are but also what they mean for you as you travel along your personal life path. In Part 1, you will explore what an aura is and how it works, and learn about the nine main aura colors (along with the additional colors that can appear in an aura). You will take an in-depth quiz to discover your aura colors and learn how to see your aura both visually and emotionally. Then, in Part 2, you will dive into the details of your aura. You will see how it presents itself in the main areas of your life: your authentic self; your spirituality; how you communicate; your relationships with family, friends, and romantic partners; your mental health; your physical health; your career and finances; your personal style; and your favorite ways of getting creative and having fun. You'll embrace your aura through activities such as:

+ Taking an energy inventory
+ Creating a sacred aura space

+ Speaking kindly to your aura

+ Hosting an aura game night

+ And more!

As you become familiar with your aura, be sure to visit the final section for insight and easy steps for how and when to cleanse your aura. This will be an important practice for maintaining a healthy, vibrant aura and protecting your energy moving forward.

Your aura has placed itself in all areas of your life, and through this book, you will begin to see its colors shine!

PART 1

understanding your aura

Validating who you are and embracing that unique self in every part of life are the gifts that come with understanding your aura colors. In this part, you will learn more about what an aura is and how it functions to help you live your best life. You will be able to distinguish between inauthentic and authentic energies and understand why you may have worn some energies in the past that weren't your own. Then you will explore each of the nine main aura colors and other colors that can appear in an aura. In addition to finding yourself described in these pages, you may also recognize close friends, family, and significant others in the different colors. After this overview of aura colors, it will be time to take the provided quiz to find out what color or colors your aura is. This quiz is designed so that the color explored in each set of questions won't be revealed until you are ready to find out your results. This way, your answers won't be influenced by how you may feel about certain colors. This part of the book ends with guidance on how to see and feel aura colors with your physical eyes and other senses. Come back to this part as a reference as you deepen your understanding of your auras and the auras of those around you.

What Is an Aura?

Your aura is an energetic signature all your own: a unique vibration that is wholly you. This powerful essence surrounds you and, without saying a single word, serves as your introduction to the world around you. Just as no two thumbprints are the same, your aura is distinct, setting you apart from anyone else who has been or ever will be. Your aura is also colorful, and the colors present in your aura reflect personality traits, skills, emotions, and imprints of the experiences you've had in life.

Although many people don't see auras in their everyday life, we can all perceive the auras of others—often without even trying. They make themselves known in the way a person makes you feel when they walk into the room, or how the mood of a place or situation is affected by someone.

HOW DO AURAS WORK?

Although merely perceiving auras can give you insights into a person, place, or experience, intentionally tuning in to and looking for auras opens up a much deeper path of understanding.

Your aura is the way in which you are energetically programmed to carry out your important life work. A part of your spiritual body—the body that can navigate between this world and the next—provides messages and information. These can include what your purpose is in this life and how you can best insert yourself into workspaces, relationships, friendships, and limitless other contexts to be valued, helpful, and fulfilled. When you allow yourself to be familiar with and flow with this authentic energy, life immediately makes more sense. By understanding that you are essentially telling a story to everyone you meet through your energy at all times, you can become a more active storyteller, writing the narrative *you* want for your life through that unique energy that surrounds you.

THE AUTHENTIC SELF AND THE AURA

As mentioned previously, your aura reflects skills and traits that are unique to you. When honored and nurtured, these can assist you in living the most authentic version of your life. In our world, however, we are often taught for various reasons to go against who we authentically are in favor of social norms and expectations. Perhaps you've been taught that spending alone time is antisocial instead of much-needed reflective self-care. Maybe you have been told that speaking up around others is rude rather than a positive example of your natural leadership abilities. These situations promote what is called an "inauthentic aura": an aura someone wears out of the belief that they won't be successful in life if they don't follow certain expectations. It takes a great deal of energy to wear an aura that isn't true to who you are, and it is a difficult mask to maintain.

When you understand and work with your true aura, you realize that living outside the lines is actually how you thrive; it's how your authentic self shines through. Additionally, choices made in auric alignment just look and feel better on those who make them. These people seem more confident in who they are and sure of their goals and desires, and they inspire others to learn more about themselves. They look and act as if they are on this planet doing what they were made to be doing because they *are*. And the way they got there was by making choices aligned with their authentic auric energy.

As you begin your journey of auric self-discovery in this book, your authentic aura will make itself known loud and clear. The changes that come with dropping who you thought you were and embracing the truest essence of yourself can be uncomfortable or surprising at first, but they will ultimately feel right. The world you know is about to shift as you delve into your aura.

The Aura Colors

There are nine main aura colors, usually found in a combination with one to two other aura colors in your energy field. The way they interact is unique to you. Understanding that one color may be more dominant than the other during certain times in your life will shed light on how and why you use them. Following the nine main colors are additional colors that can further individualize your aura. Keep reading to learn more about the different aura colors.

THE NINE ESSENTIAL AURA COLORS

These nine essential colors are the ones that present themselves most often in auras. Seeing what you relate to, and what you don't, is important in discovering the inner workings of your aura.

• • • • • RED • • • • •

Red auras are strong and assertive natural leaders. They need to be in charge and are often well respected by those they manage. Red auras regularly find themselves saying what needs to be said, however uncomfortable it may be, for the purpose of speaking the truth. They can feel responsible for upholding the moral standards of society. Red auras are good at selling others on their ideas and motivating a team to get a task done. They work well under pressure and can sometimes get loud and aggressive when they need to drive a point home. Driven solidly by logic, reds are all about reasons for doing things. They don't like emotion to cloud their vision. Red auras have good natural instincts and are very protective of their inner circle. They love a good risk and will thrive on adrenaline both in business and in life; they have a competitive edge, and their way of showing love is never going easy on anyone in life. Red auras create places to feel the pressure they crave so as to be constantly evolving into a better version of themselves. Staying active, challenged, and in high-energy contexts forges their aura into the efficient and powerful foundation they know others need to feel safe and find inspiration within.

- ✦ **Key Traits:** Motivated, ambitious, and character-driven.

- ✦ **Aligned Jobs:** Police officer, firefighter, serviceperson, salesperson, entrepreneur, manager, team leader.

- ✦ **Preferred Fitness Activities:** Weight lifting, cardio, high-intensity interval training (HIIT).

- ✦ **Compatible Romantic Partners:** They are good with empath energies as partners. Blue, indigo, and purple auras are a great fit.

- ✦ **Biggest Concern:** Injustice.

· · · · · BLUE · · · · ·

Blue auras are loving and healing people. When blue auras give to others, they connect with the divine. By doing so, they feel a sense of purpose in their life that fulfills them. Blue auras are typically in positions where they become caregivers. They are empaths, which means they feel others' feelings and pain strongly and are compelled to help. Blue auras will end up feeling responsible for the pain they see in the ones they attempt to heal and, therefore, have to watch their energetic health. They can blame themselves when the person, situation, or environment they know is hurting doesn't improve. Blues, over any other aura color, need to cleanse themselves with meditation, salt baths, and sometimes therapy. It's hard for someone with a blue aura to prioritize their needs over another's because of their innate selflessness. Blue auras have a hard time receiving even though they are very adept at giving. They tend to be extremely difficult to shop for, as they truly never want anything for themselves.

+ **Key Traits:** Healing, kind, and helpful.

+ **Aligned Jobs:** Teacher, therapist, nurse, office manager.

+ **Preferred Fitness Activities:** Walking, any activity with friends.

+ **Compatible Romantic Partners:** Those who have a shared vision of family and togetherness. Blue auras work well with any aura color; they are very adaptable in love.

+ **Biggest Concern:** Making sure people feel welcome.

· · · · · · YELLOW · · · · ·

Yellow auras are naturally curious. They have an eye for detail while they look for ways to improve in all they do, and they don't mind receiving constructive criticism or self-help suggestions to do just that. Yellow auras can tackle large and overwhelming projects with ease, and they enjoy the challenge. From the outside looking in, a yellow aura can do anything and do it efficiently—almost to the point of making life look easy. They are often perfectionists and very hard on themselves. Yellow auras don't like to be out of control with their emotions, so they do sometimes come off as cool in a crisis or unemotional to others. Their self-protective logical layer attempts to filter through information before they permit an emotion to take over. They are stoic survivors and the people everyone turns to in a crisis, as they will take the lead on making calls and organizing and completing large and unpleasant or overwhelming tasks. Yellow auras often have a tougher time living in the present moment than other aura colors and need to work on that the most. They also have to be reminded to take care of their emotions, as so often they downplay them to others and themselves.

+ **Key Traits:** Curious, organized, and introspective.

- ✦ **Aligned Jobs:** Event planner, accountant, marketing positions, real estate investor or agent, corporate director, interior designer, small business owner, social media coordinator.

- ✦ **Preferred Fitness Activities:** Pilates, yoga.

- ✦ **Compatible Romantic Partners:** Someone who understands their need for order and shares their overall vision for life. They work well with green and blue auras. A relationship with a red aura can be challenging.

- ✦ **Biggest Concern:** Lack of consideration.

· · · · · **PURPLE** · · · · ·

There is a fine line between intuition and society's version of reality, and purple auras live on this line. Purple auras are artistic and creative. Their minds are constantly moving, brainstorming, and thinking of ways to facilitate growth for themselves and the world around them. Because of this and their craving for change, purple auras need outlets to distract themselves from the daily routines of life. They are rebellious and free-spirited. They don't feel a need to be in charge, but they most certainly do not like being told what to do. Purple auras are naturally more intuitive than others, as they have faith that their emotions are proof enough of whether to trust a person or situation. Purple auras feel before they know and are often correct; therefore, they nurture a confident relationship with their natural instincts. Purple auras often attract attention and have what is referred to as the "it factor," which makes them stand out in a crowd. Purples learn to get used to this constant attention; many in the entertainment field have this color aura. Purple auras have a hard time sticking to one career in their lifetimes, as they love to spiritually evolve via challenging life situations. They do have to watch out for self-destruction, as they can use it as a quick substitute for a life change.

+ **Key Traits:** Creative, eccentric, and nonjudgmental.

+ **Aligned Jobs:** Freelance writer, performance entertainer, artist.

+ **Preferred Fitness Activities:** Dancing, group fitness.

+ **Compatible Romantic Partners:** Strong-minded partners who can challenge and inspire them. They work well with passionate red auras but can find other purple auras difficult to have long-lasting relationships with.

+ **Biggest Concern:** Stagnancy.

· · · · · **GREEN** · · · · ·

Green auras have a content and solitary vibration. Even when surrounded by lots of people, greens seem to exist in their own reality, separate from everyone else. Guided by solid logic and an unearthly ability to separate emotion from any decision-making process, green auras are strategic thinkers. They connect to their spiritual well-being through a passionate application of their knowledge to out-of-the-box, challenging projects. Green denotes an inherent ingenuity and mental capacity, but these qualities need to be constantly tapped into. Therefore, many green auras are workaholics. Without a purpose, they can become robotic and completely detached from themselves and their spiritual and emotional relationships. Green auras are interested in making a difference, fixing what is broken, and creating innovative ways for world systems to run more efficiently. They have a global awareness and can objectively see the big picture of any situation, making them amazing visionaries. They're very earth-based, find comfort in scientific research, and are often strong advocates for conservation. Green auras are amazing at seeing things for what they are and are good at sometimes using logic to convince others of the way things should be for everyone.

+ **Key Traits:** Intelligent, solitary, and systematic.

+ **Aligned Jobs:** Architect, engineer, CFO, scientist, media producer.

+ **Preferred Fitness Activities:** Hiking, running, golf.

+ **Compatible Romantic Partners:** Independent partners who can understand and support their visions. They work amazingly well with yellow and indigo auras.

+ **Biggest Concern:** Waste.

· · · · · INDIGO · · · · ·

Indigo auras are capable of viewing and experiencing everyone's point of view so clearly that it makes them feel like they're responsible for the happiness of those around them. Indigo auras can energetically feel the inner traumas that others hide, forget about, and build walls around. They fixate on these wounds in others and will change their own behavior to accommodate them and, in some way, attempt to heal them. The energy required to do this is intensely overwhelming; therefore, indigo auras must check in with who they are, not just who they are tapping into. They often need long periods of time alone to redraw and fortify their energetic boundaries. When an indigo aura pushes themselves to be in the frequencies of others too often, they can suffer physically, mentally, and spiritually. The journey for the indigo aura is about taking the time to see and validate their feelings in this lifetime. Indigo auras are gifted with analyzing behavior and creating a way for others to tap into what they have picked up on. Because they can see all sides of a situation, their gift is perspective. Dusting off the expectations of others and really getting to know oneself is a lifetime challenge for the indigo aura, making it essential to block out negative people and situations so as not to absorb that energy.

+ **Key Traits:** Introverted, compassionate, and highly sensitive.

+ **Aligned Jobs:** Specialty therapist, nonprofit coordinator, hospice nurse, animal rescuer.

+ **Preferred Fitness Activities:** Solitary exercise, nature walk, swimming.

+ **Compatible Romantic Partners:** Strong personalities who are independent in nature. They get along well with green auras but can find other empath aura relationships, such as with blue and indigo auras, difficult to navigate.

+ **Biggest Concern:** Miscommunication.

· · · · · PINK · · · · ·

Pink auras are optimistic about everything. The energy color itself has been ingrained into the collective consciousness with idioms such as a "rosy personality" or someone who looks at life through "rose-colored glasses." They tend to be positive and kind—people who are idealistic even in a situation that is well past redeemable to the rest of the world. Because of this, pink auras are often ridiculed in society as being silly, over the top, unrealistic, naive, and having their head in the clouds. They are seen as fools by those who are cynical of their authenticity. Pink auras are compassionate, very family-oriented, and hopeless romantics. They truly believe in the unequivocal good of others and in humanity. They can come across as superficial simply because they do enjoy looking nice, being attractive, and seeking beautiful things to surround themselves with. A pink aura's motivation is to see the beauty of the world consistently encompassing them. Though pink auras are prone to being misunderstood, they're loyal friends, and they choose consistently to believe that beyond the harsh "reality," there is good and beauty around us and that by being the eternal optimist, they keep that light burning for everyone else.

+ **Key Traits:** Romantic, innocent, and childlike.

+ **Aligned Jobs:** Performer, influencer, social media marketing.

+ **Preferred Fitness Activities:** Integrating activity into playful ventures.

+ **Compatible Romantic Partners:** Personalities who understand and protect their idealistic views. They work great with yellow and purple auras.

+ **Biggest Concern:** Negativity.

· · · · · TURQUOISE · · · · ·

Like pools of water, turquoise auras are naturally gifted reflectors, able to hold an image of anyone they spend time with and reflect back what they see in their own mimicked mannerisms or patterns. This allows them to show the people around them whatever it is they need to see in order to heal or fix an issue. Because of this amazing gift, turquoise auras are often incredibly confused about what direction they should be taking in life and what interests actually belong to them. They can feel ignored by others, totally unseen by the people they so closely study and assist. Identity can be a journey for the turquoise aura; to find themselves, they must travel inward rather than along any path deemed traditional by societal standards. Turquoise auras are remarkably flexible and can fit into the mold of any human condition. They are also incredibly intuitive and empathic, and because of this, are often healers of some kind. Many turquoise auras find their life purpose healing in the spiritual realms. Of all the aura colors, they have the fewest number of boundaries toward others' emotions and realities.

+ **Key Traits:** Old soul, spiritual, and reflective.

+ **Aligned Jobs:** Energy healer, doula, acupuncturist, aromatherapist.

+ **Preferred Fitness Activities:** Meditation, stretching, water aerobics.

+ **Compatible Romantic Partners:** Open-minded, compassionate partners. They work well with green, blue, and pink auras.

+ **Biggest Concern:** Being ignored.

· · · · · ORANGE · · · · ·

Orange auras represent the epitome of change. They invoke all things bold, new, and different and carry that inspiration wherever they go. This is paired with strong universe manifestation powers. It seems as if just by thinking something, they can create it in their reality. Orange auras often have high motivation and demand spaces in which to enact it. They don't fear what most do; in fact, they run toward it full speed ahead. Their dogged ambition attracts the admiration of the multitudes. They are often challenging to interpret even though they may present themselves as being extremely transparent. This mysterious charisma is the way by which they are able to charm their dreams into reality. When orange auras don't feel in control of their ability to create, they can become anxious and intense. Over time, orange auras can feel angry and irritable in this situation, as this color is meant to keep moving through the energy field of the universe and not experience a lot of stagnation. Therefore, people with this aura color tend to have many projects running at once and are often the center of multiple influential social circles. Orange auras are very concerned with how others perceive them, almost to the point of focused obsession. Those carrying the orange aura are detail-oriented, prefer to work alone, like to be in charge, and are creative problem-solvers.

+ **Key Traits:** Focused, enigmatic, and energetic.

+ **Aligned Jobs:** Entrepreneur, business development specialist, investor.

+ **Preferred Fitness Activities:** Being busy, cardio.

+ **Compatible Romantic Partners:** Partners who share in their vision and support it fully. They get along very well with indigo and blue auras.

+ **Biggest Concern:** Naysayers.

ADDITIONAL AURA COLORS TO KNOW

The nine aura colors of red, blue, yellow, purple, green, indigo, pink, turquoise, and orange in combinations of two or three make up most auras. There are also additional aura colors that can make an appearance to create nuanced messages for the person who wears them—and for those who can see and interpret them.

+ **Brown:** Down-to-earth people who crave self-sufficiency, clean living, and personal responsibility. This color in the aura often reveals a strong yet stubborn adherence to strict personal principles. Typically found with the green aura color, it can highlight a resistance to outside perspectives regarding the choices one has already made.

+ **Tan:** Hardworking individuals who have temporarily conceded about progressing or changing their mind. This color in the aura shows a sort of elective pause on the development of new ideas and opportunities that would shift focus off the tasks at hand.

Often found with the yellow and green aura colors, it can reiterate a need to stick to the basics and not get too creative in looking for solutions in life.

+ **Silver:** Incredibly intuitive and high-vibrational people who see beyond the limits of human life and seek wisdom in the worlds beyond their own. This color in the aura signifies a pursuit of wisdom that can help humanity as a whole. People with this color often have interests in science, energy, and astronomy.

+ **Gold:** Spiritual teachers who have been deemed ambassadors of high-vibrational messages. People with this color in their aura are often selfless leaders, willing to throw their lives on the line for the ideals they value. They see a bigger picture that rests beyond the limits of an earthly timeline and find their true work to be done in the ripple effects of their teachings and actions for years to come.

+ **White:** Pure and kind beings who are filled with unconditional love and an abundant amount of patience. This aura color usually surrounds young children and reappears when one becomes elderly. It signifies an understanding that the ethereal realm rests within us, and these people have the unique ability to interact with this realm so as to bring it to those who have lost its touch.

+ **Rainbow:** Creative individuals who seek unity of the physical and spiritual planes. This color in the aura reflects an attachment to past lifetimes not of a human nature and their ability to transfer and channel lessons from other planes into the human experience.

+ **Crystal:** Empathic people who bring the lessons of higher realms into the human world. This color denotes a strong connection with life-forms not of human nature and a dedication to becoming an ambassador for a world free of fear and turmoil.

+ **Black:** This rarely seen color forms when an individual's intensity has reached a toxic and unhealthy level. They see the world clearly but only through a lens of incredible pessimism and darkness. This color can be cleared up in the aura through one's attention to self-healing.

Quiz: What Is Your Aura?

This quiz is about you—the real you, not the you who you want others to see or wish you would be. Understanding your authentic aura can help you achieve everything you hope for and dream of in this life, but it begins with an honest look at your energy. Oftentimes, your authentic energy can be silenced for various reasons. In this quiz, let it free. There are no correct answers. Take a few moments to clear your thoughts before you begin.

To know your aura, complete the following steps:

1. Read through each question carefully. Check off the box that best applies to you (agree, neutral, disagree).
2. After completing each group of questions, multiply the number of "agree" check marks by 2, "neutral" check marks by 1, and "disagree" check marks by 0. Add up these sums for a final score in that group.
3. When you are finished answering and scoring each group of questions, move on to the "Scoring the Quiz" section for your results.

1. Being alone for me is healing; it's when I can feel free to be myself.

   ○ Disagree   ◉ Neutral   ◉ Agree

2. I love people, but their energy tires me; I am always tapping into their thoughts and emotions.

   ○ Disagree   ◉ Neutral   ◉ Agree

3. My ideal job is a one-on-one position in which I can really make a difference to someone.

   ○ Disagree   ◉ Neutral   ◉ Agree

4. Bright lights are the worst; my home is always dimly lit.

   ○ Disagree   ◉ Neutral   ◉ Agree

5. Confrontation paralyzes me; I cannot be around it.

   ○ Disagree   ◉ Neutral   ◉ Agree

6. At a party, I find myself socializing more with kids and pets than the adults around me.

   Disagree   Neutral   Agree

7. With friendships, it's about quality over quantity for me. I invest a lot of myself in those I love; therefore, I have to limit the amount I give.

   Disagree   Neutral   Agree

8. I can tell what people want and need without even speaking to them; I can pick up on their energy cues easily.

   Disagree   Neutral   Agree

9. I have to be very careful what I read about and watch in the media; things stay with me and affect me for a long time.

   Disagree   Neutral   Agree

10. I prefer home workouts to exercising in public.

   Disagree   Neutral   Agree

DISAGREE: _____ x0   NEUTRAL: _____ x1   AGREE: _____ x2   = _____

1. People often think of me as naive or immature, but I just can easily find the silver lining in any scenario.

    ◯ Disagree   ◉ Neutral   ◉ Agree

2. I love to set up moments for myself and the people I love that can feel like escaping from reality.

    ◯ Disagree   ◉ Neutral   ◉ Agree

3. I can be accused of being superficial, but I simply enjoy nice things.

    ◯ Disagree   ◉ Neutral   ◉ Agree

4. I connect with myself by being playful and silly; I love to have fun.

    ◯ Disagree   ◉ Neutral   ◉ Agree

5. Being active for me is a day of shopping or visiting a theme park.

    ◯ Disagree   ◉ Neutral   ◉ Agree

6. I show love to others by trying to make their life magical.

         ○ Disagree   ○ Neutral   ○ Agree

7. I love things that are fantastical and impractical.

         ○ Disagree   ○ Neutral   ○ Agree

8. When I experience confrontation, I go into myself and block everything and everyone out.

         ○ Disagree   ○ Neutral   ○ Agree

9. I am really good at adding magical elements to any event; an ice cream bar or a photo booth is the icing on the cake at any gathering.

         ○ Disagree   ○ Neutral   ○ Agree

10. A huge pet peeve of mine is a budget; I detest having limitations on creating beautiful moments.

         ○ Disagree   ○ Neutral   ○ Agree

DISAGREE:_____ x0   NEUTRAL:_____ x1   AGREE:_____ x2 =_____

1. I find myself in situations where I am helping others; it seems natural for me to take on that role.

    ○ Disagree   ◉ Neutral   ◉ Agree

2. I love to feed people and make sure they are comfortable in my home.

    ○ Disagree   ◉ Neutral   ◉ Agree

3. I am always giving to others, yet I feel taken for granted a lot in my life.

    ○ Disagree   ◉ Neutral   ◉ Agree

4. Being active for me is a walk with a friend or running around doing errands; I don't like very challenging workouts.

    ○ Disagree   ◉ Neutral   ◉ Agree

5. I am more comfortable being a helper than a leader.

    ○ Disagree   ◉ Neutral   ◉ Agree

6. I attach sentimental value to objects, making it very hard to throw anything out.

◯ Disagree   ◯ Neutral   ◯ Agree

7. At a party, I find myself seeking out anyone who looks uncomfortable and befriending them.

◯ Disagree   ◯ Neutral   ◯ Agree

8. I can feel invisible in life, as if people don't notice me the same way I notice them.

◯ Disagree   ◯ Neutral   ◯ Agree

9. Children and animals seem to like me and come to me more than other people.

◯ Disagree   ◯ Neutral   ◯ Agree

10. Confrontation is very uncomfortable to me; therefore, I end up being a peacemaker.

◯ Disagree   ◯ Neutral   ◯ Agree

DISAGREE:_____ x0   NEUTRAL:_____ x1   AGREE:_____ x2   =_____

1. I enjoy order to things; I love organizing and creating flow and systems where there is chaos.

   ○ Disagree   ◉ Neutral   ◉ Agree

2. People can perceive me as being cold, but it just takes me a moment to digest new information and create a response.

   ○ Disagree   ◉ Neutral   ◉ Agree

3. I am the one who is called in any crisis. I have a calm presence, and I know how to get things done.

   ○ Disagree   ◉ Neutral   ◉ Agree

4. My phone has a speed dial list of many different contacts for many different scenarios. People are always asking me for recommendations!

   ○ Disagree   ◉ Neutral   ◉ Agree

5. I don't go on a trip without every detail completely planned out.

   ○ Disagree   ◉ Neutral   ◉ Agree

6. Being active for me is a focused and difficult class such as Pilates or hot yoga.

   ○ Disagree   ◉ Neutral   ◉ Agree

7. Sitting down is difficult for me; my mind has a running list of things to get done.

   ○ Disagree   ◉ Neutral   ◉ Agree

8. It can be very hard for me to get past my perfectionism at times; I am very self-critical.

   ○ Disagree   ◉ Neutral   ◉ Agree

9. I am very curious, and I love to learn new things all the time.

   ○ Disagree   ◉ Neutral   ◉ Agree

10. Confrontation is not exactly fun for me, but I often end up as the mediator in a conflict.

   ○ Disagree   ◉ Neutral   ◉ Agree

DISAGREE: _____ x0   NEUTRAL: _____ x1 AGREE: _____ x2 = _____

1. I don't mind being alone; in fact, I prefer it.

   ◯ Disagree   ◯ Neutral   ◯ Agree

2. Nature is very healing to me, and I enjoy being immersed in it.

   ◯ Disagree   ◯ Neutral   ◯ Agree

3. Science makes sense to me, and I like to learn how things work.

   ◯ Disagree   ◯ Neutral   ◯ Agree

4. I don't like to hire anyone to do anything I can learn to do myself.

   ◯ Disagree   ◯ Neutral   ◯ Agree

5. I am able to separate from my emotions and keep them from influencing my decisions.

   ◯ Disagree   ◯ Neutral   ◯ Agree

6. I don't do confrontations. If someone doesn't understand me, I can easily walk away.

   ○ Disagree   ◐ Neutral   ◐ Agree

7. Uneducated claims are a huge pet peeve; I can't help but argue with anyone who promotes them.

   ○ Disagree   ◐ Neutral   ◐ Agree

8. I am a good listener, and I strive to solve problems efficiently.

   ○ Disagree   ◐ Neutral   ◐ Agree

9. Silence doesn't bother me. People I am close to understand this and don't find it awkward.

   ○ Disagree   ◐ Neutral   ◐ Agree

10. I am very interested in how things work and how they can work better. I find myself reworking how established systems could improve.

   ○ Disagree   ◐ Neutral   ◐ Agree

DISAGREE:_____ x0   NEUTRAL:_____ x1   AGREE:_____ x2   =_____

— 6. —

1. I value character traits in myself above all else. I strive to be just and do the right thing even when others disagree.

    ○ Disagree   ◉ Neutral   ◉ Agree

2. Being active for me is about getting a good sweat going; I like to push myself.

    ○ Disagree   ◉ Neutral   ○ Agree

3. Confrontation doesn't upset me; when it is necessary to speak up, I will do so.

    ○ Disagree   ◉ Neutral   ◉ Agree

4. Working for myself is the ultimate goal; I dislike answering to a boss.

    ○ Disagree   ◉ Neutral   ○ Agree

5. Responsibility and leadership are things I enjoy.

    ○ Disagree   ◉ Neutral   ◉ Agree

6. I detest when others tell me what to do; I like to be the one telling people what to do.

    ○ Disagree   ◍ Neutral   ◍ Agree

7. I am fiercely competitive, and I value this in others as well. Games aren't fun unless there is a winner!

    ○ Disagree   ◍ Neutral   ◍ Agree

8. I don't enjoy small talk; I get to the point pretty quickly.

    ○ Disagree   ◍ Neutral   ◍ Agree

9. Challenges in life drive me; I want to see how far I can go.

    ○ Disagree   ◍ Neutral   ◍ Agree

10. New situations are exciting as long as I feel in control.

    ○ Disagree   ◍ Neutral   ◍ Agree

DISAGREE:_____ x0   NEUTRAL:_____ x1   AGREE:_____ x2 =_____

— 7. —

1. My image is of the utmost importance to me; how others view me matters.

    ○ Disagree   ◐ Neutral   ◐ Agree

2. Ambition is something I have a lot of, and I don't let anything get in my way.

    ○ Disagree   ◐ Neutral   ◐ Agree

3. The word "no" doesn't exist for me; I push things to the limit in life.

    ○ Disagree   ◐ Neutral   ◐ Agree

4. Winning for me is the most important; I'll win at any cost.

    ○ Disagree   ◐ Neutral   ◐ Agree

5. Selling ideas or products is fun for me; I am good at getting people to agree with what I have to say.

    ○ Disagree   ◐ Neutral   ◐ Agree

6. I connect well with others; they find me charismatic and charming.

○ Disagree   ◐ Neutral   ◐ Agree

7. I love change when it favors my position in life.

○ Disagree   ◐ Neutral   ◐ Agree

8. I enjoy confrontation because it's an opportunity to get people to pay attention to what I have to say.

○ Disagree   ◐ Neutral   ◐ Agree

9. The more I think of myself, the more others will think of me.

○ Disagree   ◐ Neutral   ◐ Agree

10. Chaotic environments are ones I thrive in.

○ Disagree   ◐ Neutral   ◐ Agree

DISAGREE:_____ x0   NEUTRAL:_____ x1   AGREE:_____ x2   =_____

— 8. —

1. When someone tells me what to do, I have the desire to do the exact opposite.

   ○ Disagree   ◉ Neutral   ○ Agree

2. I cannot stand boredom; I am always ready to do something fun and exciting.

   ○ Disagree   ◉ Neutral   ○ Agree

3. Change is interesting to me; I don't fear it.

   ○ Disagree   ◉ Neutral   ○ Agree

4. I like to express myself in creative ways.

   ○ Disagree   ◉ Neutral   ○ Agree

5. I can't stand a traditional nine-to-five job; I need flexibility with my schedule.

   ○ Disagree   ◉ Neutral   ○ Agree

6. I love eccentric people; I am very open to new ideas.

   ○ Disagree   ◉ Neutral   ◉ Agree

7. When life gets mundane, I have to watch my subconscious ability to self-destruct in order to create interest.

   ○ Disagree   ◉ Neutral   ◉ Agree

8. While I am aware of what society deems acceptable, I find myself wanting to challenge it.

   ○ Disagree   ◉ Neutral   ◉ Agree

9. Confrontation for me is necessary at times; I like to make people uncomfortable with new ideas they fear.

   ○ Disagree   ◉ Neutral   ◉ Agree

10. The things I love the most in life tend to be artistic and outside of the norm; I don't like conformity.

    ○ Disagree   ◉ Neutral   ◉ Agree

DISAGREE:_____ x0   NEUTRAL:_____ x1   AGREE:_____ x2   =_____

1. It's hard to know what I want; it changes all the time.

   ◯ Disagree   ◉ Neutral   ◉ Agree

2. I find myself acting like anyone I spend time around.

   ◯ Disagree   ◉ Neutral   ◉ Agree

3. I love all things spiritual, and I am always seeking new knowledge in this area.

   ◯ Disagree   ◉ Neutral   ◉ Agree

4. Homeopathic remedies and alternative medicine are very interesting to me.

   ◯ Disagree   ◉ Neutral   ◉ Agree

5. Even though people think I am not paying attention, I am! I can often look distracted.

   ◯ Disagree   ◉ Neutral   ◉ Agree

6. In any conflict, I find myself trying to make sure everyone is heard equally.

⊙ Disagree　　　⊙ Neutral　　　⊙ Agree

7. I am constantly being interrupted by others, and it makes me feel invisible.

⊙ Disagree　　　⊙ Neutral　　　⊙ Agree

8. Everyone always seems to know what they want to do for a living, but I feel lost in this area of my life.

⊙ Disagree　　　⊙ Neutral　　　⊙ Agree

9. People can be alarmed by how well I know them. I tend to pick up on their core issues and don't mince words when I say them back to them.

⊙ Disagree　　　⊙ Neutral　　　⊙ Agree

10. Being active for me is anything that involves water or getting my hands dirty. I love to directly interact with the natural world.

⊙ Disagree　　　⊙ Neutral　　　⊙ Agree

DISAGREE:_____ x0　NEUTRAL:_____ x1　AGREE:_____ x2　=_____

SCORING THE QUIZ

Most people have two aura colors. While they share your energy space, they do not combine or mix; rather, they remain independent. Your top two scores reflect the two auras you have. If your score is tied on a few different aura colors, it's okay: As you practice the activities in this book, you will be able to fully discern your two authentic aura colors. Many times, the "empath" colors of blue, turquoise, indigo, and purple can seem very similar. But as you read further on in this book, the distinctions will become clear to you.

+ If you scored highest on question group 1, you most likely have an **indigo aura**.

+ If you scored highest in question group 2, you most likely have a **pink aura**.

+ If you scored highest in question group 3, you most likely have a **blue aura**.

+ If you scored highest in question group 4, you most likely have a **yellow aura**.

+ If you scored highest in question group 5, you most likely have a **green aura**.

+ If you scored highest in question group 6, you most likely have a **red aura**.

+ If you scored highest in question group 7, you most likely have an **orange aura**.

+ If you scored highest in question group 8, you most likely have a **purple aura**.

+ If you scored highest in question group 9, you most likely have a **turquoise aura**.

How to See Your Aura

Your aura does not have to be seen to be felt. Nevertheless, trying your hand at the methods described in this section can unlock deeply powerful abilities within you. You can practice these methods whenever you like and choose the ones that resonate most. Seeing auras is like working a muscle; the more you try to see an aura, the stronger the ability becomes.

VISUAL METHODS

Visually seeing the aura is a function of the third eye, and with much use and practice, this divine sight becomes as reliable as your physical sight. As you begin using these visual methods for seeing the aura, be patient with yourself. You may find the images to be fuzzy and fleeting at first, but with consistent practice, they will strengthen into full visualizations.

AWAKEN YOUR THIRD EYE

Your third eye, located in the space between your eyebrows, provides a special way to see things. With this eye, you can see the intangible realms of the energetic and spiritual world around you, including auras. Children have an especially well-developed third eye and are adept at using it to engage with various forms of play, creativity, and imagination. With age, however, your third eye dims as society reinforces the need to see with your physical eyes into the physical world, limiting your full visual capabilities. You may have a more developed third eye if you can easily visualize something that is described to you or if you are able to look at a room and instantly envision it with a new coat of paint. Of course, anyone can regain the strength of their third eye with an awakening practice. Over time, using your third eye enables you to trust it just as you do your physical eyes.

Be patient with yourself throughout this practice. It can take time to clear the fog from your third eye after years of not using it.

The first step is to simply bring awareness to your third eye chakra with mindful wonder. Observing the beauty of the world and taking time to notice its nuances is how you nudge that third eye back into its power. Contemplating art instead of just walking by it, paying attention to a garden's flowers, or noticing the brightness of the embroidered details on a sweater—these are simple ways to bring about your third eye's awakening.

Once you have practiced this, you are ready for a more focused awakening. Follow these steps:

1. Sit quietly and breathe calmly in through your nose and out through your mouth, preferably with your physical eyes closed. You may want to place a crystal on your third eye space, or you may wish to press that area with a finger as you breathe.
2. While continuing to breathe, let the visions flow.
3. As the visions flow, ask yourself questions about what you are seeing. Be observational rather than active or judgmental in your visions.
4. As your visions become harder to maintain, allow yourself to gradually end the exercise.
5. Come back to awareness of your physical surroundings when you are ready.

This practice will get easier in time as your third eye strengthens. Since this is a foundational activity for being able to see auras, be sure to practice this as often as possible.

SEE AN AURA ON YOURSELF AND OTHERS

You can do this aura viewing activity either on yourself or a willing participant. If it is a participant, have them sit in front of a blank white background. If it's you, do the same but facing a mirror.

Once you or the other person is seated, create a distinction between your physical eyes and your third eye. The physical eyes need to be defocused or made to be blurry. You can do this by staring until you see nothing in particular, just blurriness all around you. Point this gaze at the top of the other person's head or the top of your head in the mirror.

As you stare, you may see their (or your reflection's) borders begin to get fuzzy, then you may see an ethereal white color emerge from them (or your reflection). This is the first layer of the aura. The longer you can hold this stare, you may begin to see other colors emerge and grow. Over time and with practice, you'll be able to hold your gaze longer and longer so as to see the aura with more clarity.

RECORD YOUR AURA

An additional practice to try as you become more adept at seeing auras is recording yourself on camera against a white background. Set your camera to record, then sit in a meditative state in front of the white background. As you begin to center yourself and stabilize your breath, visualize your energy emanating from you. Try to do this for several minutes until you feel fatigued or disconnected. When you feel ready, you can exit your meditative state and stop the recording. Watching your recording, you may be able to see your aura! You may also want to send the video to trusted people for feedback on whether they see what you see.

EMOTIONAL AND SPIRITUAL METHODS

The following are emotional and spiritual methods of interpreting auras that can make your observations and insights more attuned and powerful. Make a note to use the following skills in everyday interactions whenever you have the chance.

ASSIGN COLORS TO MOODS

Energy is everywhere, and it's not just around people. It's around moods themselves. You may feel a pink energy when walking into a child's princess birthday party or a blue vibe when meeting your friend's baby for the first time. The ability to assign colors to moods can assist you with naturally linking auras to people and the colors of auras to specific and nuanced meanings. Over time, with conscious mindfulness of associating colors to moods, you will begin to notice patterns of certain moods that feel connected to certain colors—and in those patterns, the energetic undertows of what is really going on. Perhaps you assign red to situations that are more intense and demanding, and blue to moments of sentiment and emotion. These color assignments to the moods you experience can give you an energetic briefing of what's to come so you can better prepare for it. Take note of the color associations you freely make and compare them to the aura color guides in this book. Your unique interpretations of colors and the emotions attached to them are what create a bond between you and the energy that surrounds you, allowing you more connected insight.

To do this, simply create the mental habit of thinking about what color a given situation would have. Perhaps work meetings are yellow because you sense an overall organizational flow happening, or maybe lunch with your coworkers is purple because you laugh and point out some interesting insights into what happened at that morning's work meeting. Over time, you'll find yourself walking into an unknown environment and immediately feeling its yellow or purple energy, and you will come to understand the details as to why later on.

FEEL COLORS AS VIBRATIONS

Every aura has a distinct vibration of its own, and feeling them is how you will understand their energies. Reading auras is inextricably linked to reading your own emotions. The adjectives that follow are a guide for you to use as you navigate this book. The more you familiarize yourself with these aura colors, the more you will begin to feel them and perhaps even see them in the world around you. You may begin to notice a feeling of purple color around a fun and spontaneous friend, or a feeling of yellow around a particularly organized coworker.

+ **Red:** Intense, confident, strong.

+ **Blue:** Compassionate, calm, helpful.

+ **Yellow:** Inquisitive, capable, practical.

+ **Purple:** Spontaneous, creative, intuitive.

+ **Green:** Intellectual, focused, independent.

+ **Indigo:** Analytical, mysterious, peaceful.

+ **Pink:** Joyful, innocent, naive.

+ **Turquoise:** Transcendental, abstracted, musing.

+ **Orange:** Dynamic, electric, charismatic.

The closer you get to yourself and your authentic energy, the better able you'll be to discern the nuances that distinguish each aura from another.

Taking the Next Step

Auras are more than just personality traits or frequencies that make you feel something. They are doors that, when opened, show you the most authentic parts of yourself. Coming to understand the functional uses of your aura is how you can begin to mindfully and consciously live your life to the fullest. Your aura is ready for you, so let's dive into the next step: embracing your aura!

PART 2

embracing
your aura

Your aura is waiting for you to find it where it's always been: in the details of your life. In this part, you will not only discover where your aura has been reflecting itself every day; you will also learn how to embrace it. You will understand how to work with your energy instead of against it, and you will discover any motivations you may have had to hide or ignore your aura in the past. Each of the following ten chapters will explore one key aspect of life: the authentic self, spiritualism, communication, family dynamics, mental health and well-being, physical health, platonic and romantic relationships, money and career, personal style, and creativity and fun. You will be able to see how each aura color interacts within these parts of life, both when their energy is thriving and when they are out of balance. Then you will go even deeper into self-discovery with the eight activities provided in each chapter. Taking your time with these activities is important; self-reflection is needed to successfully take the introspective road within. Be gentle with yourself and give yourself plenty of grace and gratitude for choosing this journey. Life is about to change for the better.

CHAPTER 1

· · · · · · · · · · · · ·

Auras and the
Authentic You

Society tries to tell you who you are. Beliefs are programmed into you at school and through culture, family dynamics, subconscious biases, and the judgment you experience or witness. We are taught that to survive in this world and be successful, we need to fit in. You need to find your place in an already established system, and you may have chopped off pieces of your authentic self to do just that. But your aura is a vibrant reminder of who you are; you can't destroy it or rid yourself of it. It always finds a way to let itself be known to you. It may communicate through patterns of relationships gone sour, a habit of feeling stuck at your job, or a persistent need to do something more while never quite understanding what that is. The truth is that you don't need to ignore or suppress parts of yourself to be a successful member of the world. Instead of chopping off pieces of your energetic self to fit in, you can sculpt the world around you to better accommodate your aura. The activities in this chapter will help you do just that, guiding you in getting acquainted with your authentic self and letting your aura shine.

What Your Aura Says about You

Each aura comes with unique traits that make up your authentic self.

····· RED ·····

The healthy red aura has confidence in their strong ideals. They enjoy making their points heard in ways that are well received. Red auras value logic and justice. They are very focused on respect and cannot give it unless they feel they are getting it in return. In their best light, red auras create places for others to flourish and grow under their protection and leadership. They can have healthy conversations where different points are discussed and can model effective and calm managerial, leadership, and mediating skills for others. Red auras don't enjoy anyone who comes at them with distrust or a condescending manner, and they will put people in their place if they feel the need to do so. When a red aura has imbalanced energy, they may feel like they have nowhere to put their intense creative flow. They may internalize it as rage and let it leak out as aggressive, alarming behavior that elicits distrust in those who experience it. When a red aura loses their calm, they lose their logic, and their logic is the one thing that holds their relationship with the world together. Red auras must learn how to create a sense of self-control and maintain it to always feel they are stable and heard—if not by others, then at least by themselves. Maintaining a workout regimen, being the captain of their local softball league, or helping someone willing to take good advice is how a red aura can get back on track.

····· BLUE ·····

The balanced blue aura understands that their ability to give is a gift, not an obligation. They are adept at seeing where they are needed and will effortlessly assist and support those who need it most. Blue auras know where to spend their precious energy and resources. They seek out the ones who are grateful, the innocents, and those who will benefit from the healing work the blue aura does. The blue aura needs to see the ripple effect that they can create, in which one seemingly small act of kindness in the right place expands infinitely. They are focused on making sure others feel seen, and when they are centered, they know that they can't take care of anyone else if they don't take care of themselves first. The blue aura who understands this takes time for their self-care and speaks up when they need help, boundaries, or breaks. Blue auras who struggle to balance their energy may become victims of energy vampires—those who constantly take energy by frequently needing help, healing, and a listening ear but who never benefit from it enough to get better and pay it forward. Blue auras who aren't balanced can feel as if their only worth is to give, and they will tap themselves out to the point of severe illness, both mental and physical, in an attempt to feel they have value. Blue auras can feel like a bother and therefore not express their own needs. Balancing self-care with giving to others is how a blue aura can get back on track.

· · · · · YELLOW · · · · ·

A balanced yellow aura creates opportunity where there is none and sees potential in places where others see none. They crave the opportunity to make the most of their ability to carry out complicated tasks, and they enjoy the satisfaction of a job well done. Yellow auras are hard workers who pull from their core energy a motivation that fuels them longer than most. They thrive on questions, live for the details, and find comfort in being able to create something practical, purposeful, and beautiful. They enjoy facilitating the annual bake sale, want to help their friend redecorate their home, or find comfort in taking over the finances of an elderly family member who needs assistance. Yellow auras who burn out of their energetic flow can become stressed and tired; instead of looking at the projects around them as wonderful opportunities to interact with their Higher Selves, they see them as more tiresome tasks to be done. The yellow aura who feels exhausted finds only turmoil in their persistent ability to see the details, which become nagging reminders that they aren't doing enough. Yellow auras who outsource their self-worth to the projects they feel obligated to do rather than focusing on the ones that create joy can become resentful, exhausted, and overstimulated. They can begin to procrastinate on everything in life as they surrender to their feelings of worthlessness over their growing to-do list. The yellow aura must come to understand that there is a necessary balance in their lives, and just because they can do everything and do it well does not mean they should.

· · · · · PURPLE · · · · ·

When a purple aura is in their healthiest energetic flow, they feel free. They construct a mindset that operates outside the boundaries of modern society and exist separately from the norms others seem to follow. No matter what is going on around them, the balanced purple aura keeps a sovereign space in their vibration that feels the limitless possibilities they need to be stabilized. When a purple aura has an imbalance, however, their mindset feels erratic. They try to find their freedom in places outside of themselves, seeking liberty by way of tumultuous relationships, multiple jobs, or self-destructive behavior. The balanced purple aura knows that planning too far ahead creates anxiety instead of comfort, that they make their best choices in the most chaotic of moments, and that the mistakes they make along the way are teachers rather than something to be ashamed of. They can't hold back beginning something until the timing is perfect; instead, they must always throw themselves in and learn as they go. Their ability to go for it, no matter if they are deemed ready or not, is their superpower. Falling on their face in front of others isn't something they fear; rather, it's something they can laugh at and brush off. The balanced purple aura knows that they are relatable because they own their perceived imperfections and wear them as badges of honor. Their ability to fluently articulate this to others is what creates the same freedom mindset for others to embrace.

· · · · · GREEN · · · · ·

A green aura in their full energetic force is a true idealist. Their innate ability to acknowledge yet separate the emotions that often come with difficult decisions is their mark of excellence. This skill often puts them in spaces where they are the masters of their universe. They excel in independent work fields where they can focus on and become lost in the projects they find utterly fascinating. Green auras love a research lab they can call their own, a home garage equipped with all their tools, or an office filled with the latest tech and software. They aren't afraid to explore areas that others might find too complicated to delve into. When the energy becomes imbalanced for a green aura, their ability to separate yet acknowledge emotions becomes blocked. They construct a wall around themselves, one that the feelings and perspectives of the people and things around them cannot permeate. Their once-happy workspace becomes an isolated prison where their ability to create strong logic is the jailer. Green auras who lose their energetic flow prefer reliving the same moment over and over rather than exploring anything new that may destroy their self-made fortress. The green aura must learn that self-isolation leads to stagnancy, not growth. The discovery they so love to embark on can only be fully realized when they interact with the creative outside forces that crave their attention.

· · · · · INDIGO · · · · ·

Indigo auras are thoughtful, analytical energies who enjoy deep talks and meaningful, authentic exchanges. Empathy is their superpower. Indigo auras can feel others' feelings as strongly as their own, and they can travel deep within the pain bodies (places in the body where significant traumas are held) of anyone who comes into their energetic field. While people aren't always aware of their own pain, indigo auras can find it difficult to ignore what is so plain to them. The fear of saying something that might be construed as socially inappropriate or that the other person isn't ready to hear can cause suffering in the indigo aura. The pain they so quickly gravitate toward in another can thus become their own, creating a strong imbalance in the indigo aura. When they don't feel free to say what they know to be true to facilitate healing, they can become stifled and stuck and end up avoiding situations in which they may feel the same way. The indigo aura can become reclusive, creating worlds in which isolation is preferable to feeling as if they are not allowed to fix the things they know are broken in others. Indigo auras who are balanced see that they need outlets to freely speak to the energy they pick up in another. Professions and contexts such as therapy, specialized instruction, or simply an honest conversation are where indigo auras feel most comfortable. When the indigo aura realizes that they can create contexts in which their ability to pick up and speak to the pain they feel in others is heard and valued, they feel purposeful and whole.

· · · · · PINK · · · · ·

A healthy pink aura seems to own the universe. They are seen as inspirational, joyful beings who create a sensation of wonder and happiness for all who admire them. They are uniquely able to manifest worlds of their own design and invite people to enter them. Pink auras are incredible marketers, influencers, and entertainers because they create environments people flock to be a part of. People want to know more about their unique energy signature, and they spend a lot of time wondering what they will come up with next. When a pink aura is imbalanced, however, they can begin to shut out the shared reality necessary to exist in this society. Instead of understanding how they are perceived so that they can manage their lives on their own, they can give that power to another and focus on living in a perpetual fantasy. Pink auras can be manipulated and isolated by the people who want to keep them under control rather than allow them space to evolve and grow. When they dissociate from reality, they can become angry and defensive when anyone wants to intervene on their behalf. Pink auras can be stubborn, and, when imbalanced, this quality becomes exaggerated. Pink auras come to understand that the thing the world tends to admire is often something the wrong kinds of people want to keep for themselves. The pink aura's journey to sovereignty is one that brings them the best world of all: a place where they can be exactly who they are without anyone else's influences getting in the way.

· · · · · TURQUOISE · · · · ·

A turquoise aura can handle any situation they find themselves in due to their flowing and flexible nature. When balanced, the turquoise aura finds freedom in their ability to mindfully morph into new life situations, opportunities, and environmental contexts. They tend to carry their happy, light energy into these foreign settings and find their bearings with ease. Because they know they are doing this, they can maintain their identity as they do so. The unbalanced turquoise aura, however, allows the world to shape them without their consent. They flow into situations and subconsciously take on the environment without realizing it. This leads to them feeling numb, confused about their goals, and lost as to what their life purpose is. The turquoise aura's beautiful ability to reflect energies to those who need to take a look at themselves becomes distorted and misused. They turn into the object of projection for the things that others do not wish to see. Turquoise auras can thus feel victimized, isolated, and completely ignored by the world they so readily adapt to. The turquoise aura can come to realize that they have control and power when they understand what their beautiful gift of energetic absorbency is for: to adapt to, not be evaporated into, challenges, and to find the opportunities others don't see.

· · · · · ORANGE · · · · ·

The world is for the taking, and the balanced orange aura understands this at the very core of their being. In their healthy glow, orange auras love to feel the vibrancy of the challenges that come up as they seek their goals in life, and making new goals based on where they feel underestimated gives them even more energetic flow. The orange aura burns bright, however, and without checks and balances, they can become fatigued easily. When an orange aura is unbalanced, they can begin to rant instead of inspire, feel aggressive instead of reassuring, and become defensive instead of confident. This can cause feelings of doubt among the people surrounding them—the people they need to keep their mission moving forward. Orange auras may start to have spurts of self-doubt, and because they aren't used to feeling these emotions regularly, they will have a hard time journeying through them. Orange auras will need to realize that their downtime is essential for mustering enough energy to keep their vibrant forces balanced. Much like a fire, they need constant stoking to stay as bright as they wish to be. Finding private time to really come down from their persistent energetic highs and ponder their lows is important for the orange aura's endurance.

embracing your aura

Learn Your "Like" ·········

There are things in your life you know you're good at. These are the skills you rely on to get the job done. They are the leading elements in your energy signature; they run to meet the challenges you face in life. As a blue aura, perhaps you know how to charm your way into someone's heart, or, as a red aura, you understand that your incredible confidence gives you an edge in chaotic situations.

TAKING ACTION

1. Identify one thing you like about yourself.
2. Think about all the ways this has helped you in your life.
3. Consider how this quality relates to your aura colors.
4. Ask yourself how you can use this skill in more ways than you currently do. Perhaps as a blue aura, your charming ways can assist you in making new friends, or, as a red aura, your edge in chaos could be the reason you go for the management job you've had your eye on.

Considering how these qualities assist you and connect to your authentic energy allows them even more room to develop—and provides a way to give yourself that loving self-care you deserve. Your energy wants to be seen and appreciated; it's part of who you are. This pat on the back is the motivation your energy needs to work even harder for you moving forward.

Get Uncomfortable ·········

The place you learn about yourself best is in challenging situations. You are immediately pushed—both in your limitations and your strengths. It is in these moments that your aura can show you just what you are made of. A pink aura who stands up to ridicule as they defend their fashion choices at school, a turquoise aura who silences people who try to interrupt them while they are speaking—these people are breaking out of their comfort zone to be more authentic to themselves.

TAKING ACTION

1. Choose an activity that challenges you.
2. As you complete this activity, notice the parts that give you the most anxiety. What was the reason for this anxiety?
3. Consider how your lack of comfort in this situation relates to your aura colors.
4. Make a mental note of how great you feel now that you've completed this activity and are thriving. Congratulate yourself for stepping out of your comfort zone.

Leaving comfort zones and making conscious choices to defend your energy are the moments when you step toward a healthier and happier version of you—a you who is more authentically aligned with your aura colors.

Learn Your "Dislike" ·········

We all have something about ourselves we dislike. This quality is seen as a limitation, and it is something you probably think of immediately when faced with a new situation, person, or opportunity. It's also something that can be connected to your aura colors. Perhaps as an indigo aura, you have an intense fear of public speaking, or, as a purple aura, you feel that you tend to give a little too much information in a casual conversation.

While you see it as something to hide, this quality actually points to something great about you. The indigo aura who avoids speaking up for themselves needs to learn that they have been held back by feeling others' overwhelming energies. The purple aura who overshares now sees that they're just trying to present themselves authentically for the other person's comfort. Awareness of the limitations you have been experiencing based on the characteristics of your aura can allow you to gain control and decide when to push beyond the tendencies of your energy.

TAKING ACTION

1. Identify one thing you strongly dislike about yourself.
2. Ask yourself, "How does this show up in my life and limit me?"
3. Mindfully think about how this limitation you dislike relates to your aura colors.
4. Brainstorm ways to give it room to develop, and consider how you can work around it instead of shaming it away.

There are no wrong qualities, just attention needed in the right spaces to develop them. Indigo auras armed with the understanding of why they have a hard time speaking up for themselves can plan for creating the space they need to do so. The purple aura can work on identifying the kinds of people who appreciate learning more personal details about them.

Own Your Quirks! ·········

The parts of your energy that are not as supported by society are unique and valuable pieces of you. They are how you make your mark upon the world, bring new perspectives, create change, and step outside the lines that were drawn for you. Identifying what these traits are and creating language to bolster them is how you own that energy and make it work for you. The purple aura who is dissatisfied with a nine-to-five job but understands that it is because they are best suited for irregular hours promotes their unique energy as a strength. The red aura who cannot seem to rebel against authority understands that they instead enjoy being in leadership roles.

TAKING ACTION

1. Reflect on your out-of-the-box characteristics.
2. Consider how these relate to your auric energy.
3. Create new language around these traits to explain them in different, positive ways—both to yourself and others. For example, "I am gifted at…" or "This is useful because…"

Owning these pieces of yourself instead of shunning and degrading them gives you immense power. Giving them language that propels them forward benefits not only you but every life you touch as well. The purple aura can now see that their dissatisfaction with a nine-to-five job is actually a strength when it comes to working in nontraditional environments, and the red aura can make strides to rise up to leadership positions instead of taking a stand against authority.

Find Your Happiness ·········

There is one thing in life that you may find endlessly satisfying: A moment in your day or something you look forward to that creates a feeling of joy for joy's sake. This may be something you put on a back burner in your everyday routine because it's not as "necessary" as all your other to-dos. The yellow aura won't sit down to create their family scrapbook, because they have a never-ending list of things they want to accomplish. The pink aura may decide to do something out of a sense of obligation instead of working on their new playlist. But finding happiness in life is about finding what your auric energy loves and spending more time in this space.

TAKING ACTION

1. Think about one thing you absolutely love to do.
2. Ask yourself why this activity appeals to you.
3. Consider how your answer aligns with your auric energy.
4. Brainstorm ways to create more of this joyful connection in your life moving forward.

While there are lots of things you need to do in life (including things you don't exactly want to do), creating time for your own happiness is just as crucial. Finding your happiness is about aligning with your authentic energy and giving yourself permission to prioritize yourself and expand upon your already unique signature.

Take an Energy Inventory ·········

It's easy to get lost in the routine and fast pace of daily life. In doing so, you can lose sight of what works for you and what doesn't. The parts of your life that move with flow and ease are more aligned authentically with your aura, whereas the less aligned parts require a lot of energy to deal with. The green aura who works in customer service and feels exhausted at the end of every day may prefer working alone. The orange aura who is supporting a loved one in achieving their dream may feel lost in going after their own. Life is full of challenges, yet it's easy to make things harder on ourselves by doing things that don't align with our auras, leading to stress, fatigue, and overall dissatisfaction.

TAKING ACTION

1. While going about your normal routine today, be observational about your energy. Ask yourself throughout the day: "Is this fun?" "Why do I like/dislike this?" "What are my motives for doing this activity?"
2. At the end of the day, reflect on what activities aligned with your aura and what activities didn't, based on how you felt energetically when performing each task.

When something takes you away from your authentic auric alignment, it takes you away from your connection to yourself. Simply identifying these more difficult spaces in life can assist you with making choices that create more flow, ease, and success.

Do a Crisis Critique ·········

The role you take on during a crisis tends to highlight your authentic auric energy. When the world around you seems to fall apart, the words you use, jobs you try to fill, and ways you help are all in line with your innate self. The yellow aura who gets busy tying up the loose ends no one else is thinking of, or the blue aura who begins to take care of everyone's immediate needs for comfort are examples of knee-jerk reactions in a crisis that show us who we truly are.

TAKING ACTION

1. Think back to the last time there was a crisis when you had to assist in some way.
2. What were your immediate reactions, thoughts, and actions?
3. How do these reactions, thoughts, and actions align with your aura?
4. Mindfully analyze how you felt during this crisis. Where do you feel you did well? Where do you feel you could have done more?

Crisis times are not always pleasant to think about, but understanding what you do and how you contribute in a crisis will help you bring more of that aid to future situations where you are needed. Your specific role is unique and necessary. No one can do everything in a time of crisis, and your contribution matters.

Capture the Moment on Camera ·········

Your authentic self isn't just an action or a definition; it's a feeling. Capturing that feeling in a bottle isn't exactly possible, but getting it on camera is. As you go about finding your authentic auric energy, you are bound to be overcome with a feeling of something bigger than you—the connection that exists between you and the universe. The turquoise aura feeling grounded in the woods or the indigo aura splashing happily in the waves may feel connected to the very heart of the universe itself.

TAKING ACTION

1. Take a selfie or a picture of the environment you are in during a joyful moment when you feel totally aligned with yourself and the universe as a whole.
2. Place this photo where you can see it often. Set it as your phone background or post it on a bulletin board or the fridge.
3. Every time you look at the photo, think about how far you've come in reaching your authentic self and how this feeling is the goal.
4. Give yourself gratitude for the beautiful energy you allow to live within you. You may repeat, "I am filled with self-love!" or some other phrase you design.

Capturing a moment of pure joy and alignment is a way to capture a little piece of yourself. Seeing it is a reminder of the feeling you have when you are connected to the energy that feeds you, gives you unconditional love, and validates who you authentically are. The knowledge that no one can shake who you are, no matter what happens, is precious.

CHAPTER 2

· · · · · · · · · · · ·

Auras and Spiritual and Psychic Connections

Your spiritual body, as you will come to see, is just as essential as your physical one. Your spiritual body houses your aura and is a sort of extension of you into the various unseen planes of the universe where ethereal wisdom and guidance are found. You may call this guiding wisdom Spirit, God, the divine, or any other word that feels right. Your aura allows you to experience spiritual connection with this force and send and receive psychic messages to and from it. How does this work? Everything in the world around you gives off a frequency, and your aura is constantly communicating with these frequencies. It is the attention to these frequencies that will release your heightened ability (or intuitive power) to decipher and work with them. The gifts you inherently have through your intuition can be unlocked even further as you journey into your aura and its connection to spirit and psyche. Through delving into your aura, you can manifest intuitive abilities in clairvoyance (clear seeing), clairsentience (clear feeling), and claircognizance (clear knowing). In this chapter, you will get to know your spiritual self and expand your connection with the universe around you.

What Your Aura Says about You

Each aura connects to spirituality in unique ways.

····· RED ·····

Red auras value logic over anything else, and a common error they can make is to think that logic is somehow separate from intuition. The way into the red aura's sixth sense comes by way of instinct or a gut feeling. They may describe it as a primal knowing or an obvious tell based on consistent logical strategies they have come to rely on their entire lives. A healthy dose of skepticism moves the red aura to sit back and observe all the people they meet, always looking for the angle at which others operate. In their attempt to study behavior and find underlying motivations that may not be in line with the words they hear, they are, in fact, connecting with their intuitive self. They can pick up on psychic feelings and vibrations but label them as character flaws or simply a general personal dislike. They can use all their cues to simply know, which is a form of claircognizance, or "clear knowing." In communicating with the paranormal or intelligent energies that attempt to cross into our earth planes, red auras will often experience more physical feelings. Feeling physically ill, nauseated, and sweaty may all be ways a red aura senses they are not alone—when, for all "logical" purposes, they are. The red aura needs to believe to see, but once they do, it's hard to sway them from their own spiritual experiences.

· · · · · BLUE · · · · ·

Blue auras are conduits for spirit energy, and they readily make themselves available for this in any way they can. Creating opportunities to comfort those in a crisis, give out something needed, or simply hug a person who feels lonely in this world is how they make this spiritual connection. Blue auras live to feel "the glow"; that is, the feeling they sense someone receiving when they've been validated, seen, and shown unconditional love for no other reason than pure no-strings-attached kindness. That glow is Spirit, or the intelligent force that governs the universe. Blue auras often find comfort in living among energies not of this plane; therefore, they often find it easy to communicate with loved ones on the other side or acknowledge their angelic helpers. Blue auras do this through keeping memories alive, feeling the presence of those who've passed on, and following their intuition to ask a stranger if they need any help. In their selfless ability to help and see those who need a loving touch, blue auras are channeling the energy of the universe itself.

· · · · · YELLOW · · · · ·

There is beauty in the details—fine points in which the divine rests quietly, waiting to be noticed by the one with the discerning eye. Yellow auras see the energy of the universe in these places, connect with Spirit while they do so, and structure a world in which others can experience this same magnificence. Yellow auras like to connect to loved ones who have passed by memorializing something that was important to them for future loved ones to experience. Their intuitive voice alerts them to things that have been overlooked, as they have a bit of a detective's eye when it comes to seeing the world in puzzles, patterns, and missed opportunities. Leaving no stone unturned, they seemingly tidy up as they go, and in doing so, they reveal truth where it was once hidden. Yellow auras channel their psychic skills via their curious voice. Questions are the fuel that propels their journey. The feeling of something being off with a friend's boyfriend or a questioning feeling as they browse through accounting papers are actually the yellow aura's intuition picking up loose energetic ends that cry out to be tied. Their psychic gift grows when they follow these tugs to their sources and build their confidence to continue valuing the questions that fill their minds.

· · · · · PURPLE · · · · ·

The veil is thin between this world and the next for a purple aura. Their ability to jump into others' energies for the purpose of grasping the person's perspective is quick and often very accurate. They tend to watch others like a movie, observing and understanding but not always holding what they feel and see with the same depth of emotion that those who are experiencing it do. Because of their ability to understand perspectives without absorbing them to the point of emotional exhaustion, they hover above the emotional limitations that hold others back when delivering intuitive feelings with accuracy. Purple auras don't hesitate to say they can't trust your friend or they think the couple they just saw get married won't last more than a year. They simply know, and when proven right in time, they tend to gain more confidence in their intuitive voice. Purple auras have a better ability to see past this world and will receive visions or random "downloads" of information without even trying. They are often clairvoyant, or "clear seeing," due to their enhanced third eye abilities. Because they are so easily approachable energetically, paranormal beings tend to be very attracted to them. The purple aura has many supernatural stories and experiences, and while they know others won't ever believe them, it never shakes their own faith in what they know to be true.

····· GREEN ·····

Green auras are natural visionaries. Their way of seeing how to make the most unlikely connections or solve problems that aren't even questions yet is how they enact this skill. It's also how they connect with Spirit and demonstrate their intuitive voice. The ability to invent a tool to fix a window, calmly mediate a hostile conversation, or create an algorithm to promote their website are all green aura examples of divine connection. The space they delve into while they work is a space in which a higher power resides. Green auras are interested in the paranormal when they can document it, and therefore will decide to explore the supernatural with gadgets and technology that they feel could truly capture what others may simply call an off-putting feeling. The documentation of the sudden temperature drop in a purportedly haunted room may excite them more than actually feeling the temperature change themselves, for the green aura trusts what exists in the systems around them. Green auras know that their connection with nature is an important one, as they can match their own frequencies with the perfect vibrations of nature itself. This allows them to be even more skilled in seeing the world in the way a higher power can.

····· INDIGO ·····

Indigo auras don't fear the unknown; in fact, they prefer stepping right into it—and staying a while. Feeling the deeper and more hidden layers of other people is often how they make their way in this world. Connecting with the deeply rooted pain bodies they sense in others is where their intuitive voice takes them. Often, they find their spiritual connection strengthened when they follow this intuition and use it to heal those they can feel need it. Because of this, indigo auras are able to step into another's energy to fully comprehend their intentions and deep reasoning for doing what they do. Their empathic ability really is their psychic skill, and they understand that the other side that awaits us after this life isn't somewhere distant: It is a place we can travel to whenever we want by way of our deep emotions. In dealing with the paranormal, indigo auras are able to sense it and not always fear it. A "haunted" house or a piece of jewelry with attached energy can tug at the space they find comfort in—the one that often feels like it's in between worlds (and at times isolated). They can sense the energy of other beings who aren't exactly on our timeline or our plane of earthly existence. Just as they can pinpoint a feeling in a person in order to help and heal, they can do the same for energy that is not quite here. They trust it and follow it to meaning, which leads them to their own unique psychic voice.

· · · · · PINK · · · · ·

With their unique skill of creating a world around them that is fantastical and quasi-magical, the pink aura has a divine ability to manifest their dreams into reality. They believe what they create, and they support their visions with choices and aligned attitudes, watching in awe and delight as the universe follows that vision to what others can see as well. Pink auras have a pure intuitive sense very much like children do. They can see when someone is overworked, resentful, fearful, or insecure. They don't always have words for what they see; rather, they experience a feeling that overcomes them. Pink auras connect with the inner child of all people they meet, and their intuitive voice leads them there. This voice becomes psychic when it begins to construct realities and fantasies for that other person to experience, and it helps them connect individually with the child they have long since forgotten. Instead of sitting down and having a chat, the pink aura may take them to a place they know makes their inner child joyful. Having a party, going to an art studio, or taking the perfect picnic lunch to the beach are all ways a pink aura connects to another's ability to unlock joy. They understand that finding joy is a way to healing.

····· TURQUOISE ·····

The ability to be a conduit for energy is a turquoise aura specialty. They allow the frequencies of this world to pass through them with ease, and by doing so, an inordinate amount of information is given to them. When the turquoise aura has a better grasp of this ability, they can begin to learn how to manipulate the energy to heal others. Turquoise auras often have healing hands and can work in energy-healing modalities with great success. Doulas, energy healers, or crystal grid artists all use their intuitive energy in some form to assist people in finding their own strength. Turquoise auras are also incredibly psychic when it comes to picking up on the nuances of individual energy fields. They can take on and reflect the qualities, both good and bad, that another person needs to see, thereby creating self-awareness. The intentional turquoise can use these gifts in ways that offer honest assessments to those who appreciate their work and will benefit from it. Turquoise auras are often so sensitive to the unseen realms that they can be the first to sense a shift in the collective consciousness. When speaking about what they feel, they may sound eccentric to others at first, but through hindsight, people will see that they were in fact picking up large-scale energy shifts. Turquoise auras are like water: They need refreshing and prefer to flow rather than to remain stagnant. Working with energies and articulating what these energies are saying is a way they can spiritually cleanse themselves and others.

····· ORANGE ·····

Orange auras know people and understand how to read them with great ease. Rather than calling this an intuitive sense, they may describe it as their brilliant conversational skills or an extraordinary sales mentality. Whatever words they choose to use, they have an innate psychic ability to know how people will react *before* they do. Their intuitive sense becomes a full-blown psychic skill when they begin to use their own precognition to determine how a person will react. They then use this information to plan out a unique approach that ensures their reaction is in line with whatever the orange aura's idea is, making them very efficient at hyping people up for projects they need cooperation on. Orange auras make people feel seen, and this is because they truly do see them—not just their outsides but also their innermost feelings and fears. Orange auras speak the truth plainly, so they seem trustworthy. They know how to buddy up to everyone's energies and line up their own frequency to match these auras. In dealing with the paranormal, orange auras don't fear anything that can't touch them or their 3D world. They are less concerned with energy that comes from other places and stay focused on what affects them in the here and now. Unbeknownst to them, however, the orange aura does connect with otherworldly energy by reviving it and bringing it back to its full glory. Rebuilding an old brand or restoring the dignity of a rundown historical building are ways the orange aura interacts with the unseen realms around us all.

embracing your aura

Create Your Auric Bubble ·········

There are energies swirling around you all the time, carrying with them distinct messages they want you to hear. They will do this by latching on to your emotions, physical body, and auric energy. You may not even be aware of these energies that consistently infiltrate and drain you. Fortunately, creating a strong auric bubble of protection gives you more control over the energies that affect you. Not only will you have more of a boundary to these energies, but you will also be able to see your aura and better understand what it needs to be healthier and stronger.

TAKING ACTION

1. Close your eyes (if possible, keep them closed throughout this activity) and take a few deep breaths until you feel calm.
2. Envision a glowing light pouring into you from an unseen place outside yourself that your intuitive wisdom understands is benevolent and healing.
3. Take the time to feel and see this light filling every part of you.
4. When you are filled with this light, see it expand out of you, encasing the 6 to 12 inches of space around your body. This is the protective bubble around your aura.
5. As you look at your aura bubble, ask yourself about the colors you see. Are there any weak spots or gaps that need fixing? Send the light to those spaces and see them healed immediately.
6. When you feel the image beginning to fade, or if you simply know it's time to end, exit your meditative state.

Your aura bubble will shield you in times of distress or uncertainty. In time, you will get better at creating this auric bubble around you in any situation, even without having to meditate.

Practice Clairsentience · · · · · · · · ·

Clairsentience is the power of "clear feeling," a psychic ability to feel others' feelings and traumas. Empath auras (blue, indigo, purple, and turquoise) often have the most enhanced clairsentient abilities. It's very possible that as a blue aura, this ability is why you always know exactly how to help someone without being told, or why, as a purple aura, you tend to point out some hard truth that seems totally unexpected but not inaccurate. If you have this psychic ability, a fundamental skill is learning how to differentiate others' emotions from your own.

TAKING ACTION

1. Put your hand over your heart and close your eyes for the duration of this activity, if possible.
2. Ask yourself how you feel right now. You may have to dig deep, as feelings can hide in physical symptoms or sensations of anxiety.
3. Consider whether this feeling is yours. If not, where did it originate from?
4. When you receive your answer, gently exit the meditative state.
5. Repeat this activity several times a day until it becomes an ingrained habit.

In being able to pinpoint another's emotions and how they are separate from yours, you have incredible power. You can no longer be manipulated by others' unsaid wants and needs, you have more free will in choosing where you put your energy when helping people, and you can get to the truth of the matter more easily when assisting someone in their own pain and trauma.

Make a First Impression Prediction ·········

The way your intuitive voice speaks to you is largely ruled by your auric energy. You may feel a need to place your hands on someone in a spot where you believe they have physical pain (as a turquoise aura would), or you may sense someone has bad intentions by their body language (as a red aura may). Many times, your aura is the way by which your intuitive voice speaks to you, but because it's so normalized for you, it doesn't feel like anything out of the ordinary. Your natural inclinations, instinctual feelings, and curiosity are all ways by which your aura can alert you. Paying greater attention to your aura and the predictions and messages it brings you intuitively can help you use this skill to its full potential.

TAKING ACTION

1. Think of someone you are acquainted with.
2. Reflect on your first impression of them. What intuitive messages or feelings did you get about them, and how did you get them?
3. Determine whether the feelings, messages, and premonitions you got on your first impression turned out to be true or false.
4. Make a mental note of how you approached your first impression and connect those methods to your aura colors.

Seeing in hindsight how your intuitive feelings play out can help you use them to make stronger predictions in the future.

Connect with an Ancestor · · · · · · · · ·

The connections you have with the people who shaped your current reality can be powerful ones. Those who came before you had hopes and dreams, and they invested time and energy into them. Their stories are important, and connecting to them creates a spiritual bond between the energetic world and you. How you go about this is easier when you are directed by your aura colors. Red auras may want to look into an old family business, whereas yellow auras may decide to research and create a detailed family tree. Use your interests in this activity to strengthen that psychic bond with the other side.

TAKING ACTION

1. Choose an ancestor you would like to know more about.
2. Determine how you would like to learn more about this ancestor and start exploring. Mindfully notice how you pick up information in an energetic way, via emotions, facts, or a feeling of interest and deep knowing.
3. Reflect on how your aura is evident in the ways you research this person's story.
4. Consider what you think this ancestor's aura colors were. Why do you think they were those colors?

Continuing this energetic conversation with ancestors can have a profound effect on your life and how you view your own goals and dreams moving forward.

Ground Your Aura in Nature ·········

Nature is an incredible grounding force for coming into your full auric power. The forces of nature allow you to see yourself with great clarity so you can begin approaching your connection with self and Spirit in the way that best aligns with your aura. A green aura may love a long hike in the woods to feel their higher power, a turquoise aura may discover their passion for creating beautiful rock sculptures in their garden, and a purple aura may realize that they think more clearly when sketching a bird they see in their backyard. Your auric energy thrives in this environment, and it shapes how you interact with the natural world.

TAKING ACTION

1. Go outside and either walk around barefoot or sit somewhere that feels inviting to you.
2. As you walk or sit, look around and see what you are called to do. You may wish to lie down to see things from new perspectives, feel the need to draw or write, or simply observe your surroundings with calm curiosity.
3. Think about how what you came up with in the previous step aligns with your aura.
4. Brainstorm ways to explore yourself more regularly through the medium of nature.

Introducing yourself to nature as you are and allowing it to communicate to you with its energies strengthens your natural spiritual connection to the world around you. Grounding work feeds your soul on many levels, creating cohesion between the spiritual realm and your own self.

Communicate with the Paranormal ·········

Energy that is concentrated and left behind by a person or event is interesting to explore. Historical places with vibrational signatures of the past that you can still somehow sense or a piece of antique furniture that has an element of yesteryear still clinging to it are very enticing to your energetic frequencies. Your auric energy will automatically interact with these paranormal energies with or without your explicit knowledge. The yellow aura may experience a barrage of curious questions begging to be answered; the indigo aura may feel intense emotion that comes quickly and seemingly out of nowhere. The more you understand how your energy communicates with the unseen world, the more you can pick up the messages and insight it has to give.

TAKING ACTION

1. Choose a place or an object that has a history that intrigues you.
2. Ask what you notice about your own self when you are in its energy field. How do you feel your energy is interacting with the energy around you?
3. Reflect on how your reactions, questions, or impulses line up with your aura colors.

Energy cannot be destroyed, only transformed. Your energy is able to recognize this in the environments it travels along with you. Using it as a tool to interpret these energies can unlock a few mysteries of the paranormal world, which has an abundance of messages to share with you.

Collect Mystical Tools
for Your Aura ·········

In your journey to connecting with your auric energy, you may find that certain mystical tools assist you and provide comfort. When used properly, they uniquely celebrate and support your aura to its fullest potential. A pink aura may find comfort in their rose quartz crystal when they feel anxious or stressed, while a turquoise aura may collect various essential oils to assist in their journey to inner peace and calm. Your aura is uniquely attracted to different mystical tools. The journey you go on to discover which tools speak to your energy will provide a lot of feedback about what you already have and what you need more of in your energetic body.

TAKING ACTION

1. Visit a New Age store that carries a variety of mystical merchandise.
2. Look around thoughtfully, staying present and seeing what items genuinely spark your interest.
3. When you find yourself curious about an item, reflect on the reasons behind your interest and how this tool aligns with your aura colors.
4. Consider what this tool suggests you need support with or how it embraces what you already are.

Supporting your energy with items that validate its existence creates a stronger flow between you and your authentic energetic signature. When you see yourself and provide tools to further your progression, you are giving yourself a context in which to grow.

Make a Sacred Aura Space · · · · · · · · ·

There are places in the world where you may feel more spiritually connected than others. Perhaps it's a house of worship or the top of a hill. It could even be in your own reading nook you created just for yourself. Having a space that is sacred to you and created for your energetic body to spend time in enhances your auric vibrations. The spaces in which you allow yourself to truly open up to the communication between your auric energy and your physical self create a stronger bond, leading to a more harmonious and peaceful spiritual existence.

TAKING ACTION

1. Think of where you can create a space that is completely your own.
2. Mindfully think about what purpose this space has and how it is a sacred one.
3. Build this space using elements you feel comfortable and peaceful with, such as candles, a blanket knitted by a family member, plants, etc.
4. Reflect upon how this space and its parts align with your aura.

Spending time in your sacred space gives your energy room to heal and gain strength. A strong energy signature is one that works for you. Your sacred space is a little investment in allowing your aura to flow vibrantly.

CHAPTER 3

· · · · · · · · · · · ·

Auras and Communication

As you have learned, energy flows through you. And the way you give voice to it matters. Communication is how you verbalize the energy you want to send out to the world. It is also the way you receive others' intended messages and create connections among distinct energies. Communication is really about expressing yourself in a way you want others to comprehend and hearing what others are trying to say. It's also validating, giving yourself and those around you time to feel seen and heard. Each aura color has its own method of transmitting its energy and tapping into the energy of others. In this chapter, you will discover the communication strengths and preferences of your aura, as well as where improvements could help you communicate more effectively. You will also uncover the communication styles of other aura colors so you can factor these into your interactions. Leaning into your particular modes of expression and embracing the modes used by others will allow everyone's ideas to be heard with more acceptance, interest, and ease.

What Your Aura Says about You

Each aura communicates in unique ways.

····· RED ·····

The red aura has many ideas and enjoys an audience who appreciates their logic-based style of communicating. Often capitalizing on the fact that most people tend to sit back and let another person stand up, organize, and lead the way, the red aura automatically seems to do just that in any context they are in. They don't like ideas that aren't organically their own, and they can have a hard time hearing others' concepts no matter how good they may be. Red auras don't mind a conversation about the best way to approach a problem in life. While they often articulate their ideas with force and confidence, when self-aware, they will openly engage in a respectful conversation about alternatives or ways forward—as long as the final say always goes to them! Red auras love a healthy argument and can handle shaking hands and ending on a note of agreeing to disagree. Red auras are solutions-based people. When they hear about a problem, they automatically set themselves in line to find and foster the solution. Being around those who want to analyze feelings and sit in emotions rather than fix the perceived problem can cause them to feel frustrated and upset. Red auras must learn that they don't always have to put their leadership into action when it comes to situations that instead may require more emotional discourse.

····· BLUE ·····

Blue auras have a hard time self-advocating in their exchanges with others. While they can stick up for the wants and needs of the people around them, they can't always use their voice for themselves. Blue auras often use their communication skills for peacemaking between others in conflict. They can be energetic translators of sorts, reinterpreting the exact words someone says to make them more palatable for the opposing side to digest. Because blue auras are very good at communicating on behalf of others but have a more difficult time doing this for their own wants and needs, resentments can build. Their bottled-up feelings and unheard needs can come out in erratic ways. Blue auras can have emotional outbursts that feel out of place in the moment they are delivered. They can become triggered by one slight after years and years of suffering in silence over thousands of them. Blue auras can take what others say personally when they get to this point and may be unable to see past their own persecuted, painful feelings. They can feel victimized and sad, wanting so desperately to be seen and heard the way they see and hear others. Blue auras have to learn to give themselves that opportunity the same way they facilitate it for the people in their life. Learning to use their words to vulnerably express their own repressed feelings is essential to building the blue aura's communication skills.

· · · · · **YELLOW** · · · · ·

In a world full of nonessential details, the yellow aura knows how to slice through to the pertinent points at hand. Since they are so naturally good at this, they are often praised for it and called upon to do it in all sorts of complicated contexts. The yellow aura communicates what they see honestly and directly, and this is truly their way of showing love. Their ability to pare down an overwhelming world to a few points that are worth considering can help others immensely. Sometimes, however, the situation calls for a different type of delivery, one that yellow auras are not as well versed in. Yellow auras learn quickly that some of those details they deem "nonessential" are emotions. Because of this, they can be seen as a bit tough or hard to crack. They perceive emotions as factual pieces of information or problems that must be tackled and solved instead of being thoughtfully studied. Yellow auras can speak to themselves in a way that is just as cutting and cool, leaving them needing more nurturing than they know how to deliver. The yellow aura must learn that emotions aren't always something to rush through; rather, they can be soft, contemplative places to consider.

· · · · · PURPLE · · · · ·

The purple aura's world of constant change creates a similar communication pattern of dynamic movement. They understand it's okay to change one's mind and that change should happen often to further personal growth. The purple aura doesn't often look for one particular answer; rather, they have an intuitive understanding that in this strange world, there are an infinite number of ways to respond to a question. Purple auras enjoy the freedom of communication and therefore seek out people who are equally as fluid at accepting new ideas. They enjoy conversing with open minds, but when they meet someone who is less open, they find it very entertaining to push the buttons they so effortlessly recognize in that person. Any sort of thought, moral code, or societal belief that is widely accepted as true is fascinating to purple auras, and they often target these assumptions to test their stability. Creating a question in the minds of others is what purple auras strive for when communicating. They seek to stir things up and see if they can understand if what others feel so strongly about can be changed or moved in some way. This exchange of information energetically levels up both parties. Purple auras can sometimes take their rebellious spirit too far in discourse, where it will go from a genuine questioning to a need for discord. Purple auras need to focus on their ability to open minds and promote creativity with their style of communication.

····· GREEN ·····

As chaotic as the world may seem, green auras always find the pattern. They pay attention to the systems at play—the silent forces that guide us through principles of logic, science, and nature. Green auras attach so much meaning to these systems as sources of truth, they forget at times that not everyone can see them as clearly as they are able to. When communicating themselves, green auras can display this perception of systems around us that is so seemingly obvious to them, causing others, who cannot see as they do, to sometimes ignore or ridicule them, or even shut them out. What is considered "common sense" for many green auras doesn't always translate as such to the rest of the population, which can cause a lot of confusion for both the green aura and those they communicate with. Green auras are often loners and don't need the approval of others to feel heard or seen, but to bring education, awareness, and growth to the world around them, they need to communicate with others more effectively. Green auras who learn not only to speak about what they see and know but also to show others how to see these things are most successful in communicating. This can have a powerful effect on the people in their lives and on humanity as a whole.

····· INDIGO ·····

Feeling the deepest unspoken feelings in a person upon first interaction is automatic for the indigo aura. Therefore, ignoring these wounded pain bodies and instead making socially acceptable small talk can be extremely energetically draining for them. Their ability to communicate is grounded in deep emotional conversations, forging change through these healing and honest connections. The indigo aura finds comfort and ease with one-on-one interactions in which both parties are open to this kind of vulnerable conversation. Indigo auras can become so overwhelmed in daily exchanges that they often disappear rather than continue engaging with others. Out of fear of being seen as odd, morbid, or eccentric, they opt to avoid communicating at all, leaving others to wonder what happened to cause their sudden and unexplained exit. Indigo auras can feel others' perceptions at the same time they are expressing their own feelings, causing them to feel double the emotions. Indigo auras aren't always equipped to handle negativity, confrontation, or opinions that aren't empathic, and can find themselves at a loss for words in these situations. Writing is a good alternative for the indigo auras who lose their words in the moment they need them. The indigo aura who learns to advocate for the contexts that promote healthy communication and vulnerably explain what they can and cannot handle in more surface encounters are better able to articulate what they need to say in a world that so desperately needs to hear it.

· · · · · PINK · · · · ·

Pink auras know what it is to be dismissed and often come to expect it. They can shut out the world automatically, with little to no care for how it looks to the people around them. They will communicate by being completely themselves, oftentimes seemingly ignoring the communicative efforts made by others. When they want to create an energetic exchange between themselves and another, they invite them into their own world instead of leaving it to go live in the physical world. Pink auras don't try to be understandable; in fact, without practice, they can lose sight of what it is they need to say or do to make meaningful contact with others. Because pink auras are often told to leave behind the joyful, innocent, and childlike perception they have of the world, they self-preserve by learning to not listen at all. This leads them to distrust any method of communication around them. The pink aura who finds strength in their own perception and understands that no one can control them finds it easier to learn other ways to connect with people around them so that everyone's ideas and views are seen, heard, and shared.

····· TURQUOISE ·····

Bursting at the seams with energies that come and go as they please is how the turquoise aura knows life. Their ability to communicate goes beyond words, for their actions and treatment of others become a reflective response dictated by what each person subconsciously seeks and needs. They mirror others' true selves back to them. An awareness of this impressive energetic gift assists with their control over who they will do this for, but even so, their ability to take in all perspectives at once is overwhelming and confusing. They may begin to treat a person the way that person is treating another, or act in a way another person may find triggering due to an unhealed emotional wound. They may say things that are so deeply profound but that arrive seemingly out of nowhere, leaving the people around them unprepared and unsure of how to respond. This can cause the turquoise aura to feel judged, unheard, and even unloved. Their understanding of their communication style needs to go beyond what they say to why they are saying it and for what purpose. The turquoise aura, more than any other color, must practice self-awareness of what they want to say and continue to place themselves in loving and appropriate contexts that value their words and deeds as such.

····· ORANGE ·····

If anyone knows how to connect with a crowd, it's an orange aura. Dynamic and bold, they tend to naturally have their fingers on the pulse of the world in which they live. They understand what everyone's thinking and are able to put words to it for it to be heard and received by all. Orange auras are brilliant at making others feel seen and heard, as they can connect to that unseen part of a person who feels they have been looked over. They put words to the feelings others don't know how to express and, in doing so, make each individual feel important. Their method of communication is like anything else the orange aura does: to advance their own ideas and goals. The orange aura wants to include everyone in the process, as they inherently know that this makes the job easier. The orange aura has an authenticity to their exchanges, a feeling of a larger-than-life presence. Faith becomes part of the relationship, whereby the orange aura can do what the other person doesn't feel capable of doing. And the orange aura knows this. As they are cheered along their path, they carry with them the words of all those who feel connected because of what the orange aura says.

embracing your aura

Speak Kindly to Your Aura ·········

The way you speak to yourself matters. You may be taught to control your most repressed energies by scolding or speaking down to them in your head. Perhaps as a blue aura, your sensitivity is perceived as weakness, or, as a green aura, your ability to see the big picture makes it difficult to fit in socially. Your aura can give insight into your communication patterns and an awareness of how to strengthen and embolden them rather than belittle and repress them. In this activity, speaking to yourself in a kind manner will unlock a new pattern of communication focused on self-respect.

TAKING ACTION

1. Think of a time when you were particularly hard on yourself. What words did you say to yourself?
2. Now consider the perceived weaknesses you sought to punish in this situation. How can you relate them to your aura colors?
3. Determine how you can change those critical words to validate and showcase these qualities instead of shaming them. For example, "I love my ability to…"
4. Continue practicing these kind words any time you feel tempted to be hard on yourself.

The communication patterns in your mind are considerably the most important ones. Creating awareness and ownership over them helps you to live your most authentic life.

Study the Difficult People ·········

Life will provide challenging people we are forced to interact with at times. The ways in which we find them difficult can be traced back to parts of our own auras, which may need some energetic nurturing. Perhaps as a red aura, you find the helpful suggestions of yellow auras triggering because you may interpret them as undermining your own ideas. Or, as a turquoise aura, constantly being interrupted by the more vocal purple aura in your life can cause a feeling of anger toward your pattern of being unseen and unheard.

TAKING ACTION

1. Reflect on a difficult person in your life you often miscommunicate with. What feelings do you have when forced to communicate with this person?
2. Consider how these feelings relate to your energy in terms of perceived weaknesses, insecurities, and miscommunication patterns.
3. Think about their aura: What are its colors, and how do they play into the way this person speaks to you?
4. Consider how you can use your own authentic energy to circumnavigate these communication shortcomings between the two of you for future conversations; for example, having a predetermined line you can use with a difficult person or speaking up clearly the next time the issue arises.
5. Repeat a mantra of self-love based on whatever you feel you lack. For example: "I am heard by the universe."

The difficult people in your world can provide insight into how to improve your communication skills. When you see how a certain type of communication style upsets or stifles you, you are better able to deal with it rather than avoid it.

Awaken Your Throat Chakra ·········

You can assist your ability to create a cohesive flow between your energy and the way you express it with a throat chakra awakening exercise. The throat chakra is energy that sits around the throat, jaw, neck, mouth, and thyroid. When your throat chakra is balanced, you speak with confidence and authenticity. You can listen to others more effectively and respond in ways that create understanding among you. When this chakra is imbalanced, you may find that others misconstrue your intentions, ignore what you have to say, or find speaking with you difficult.

TAKING ACTION

1. Sit quietly and calmly, allowing yourself to breathe deeply until you settle into a peaceful state.
2. Envision a blue light sitting at the base of your throat. See it glow and grow stronger.
3. Repeat the mantra "I am authentically speaking and listening" out loud, if possible, as many times as you need to for it to feel true to you.
4. Close the activity by seeing the glow of your blue throat chakra become brighter, then fade within you once again.
5. Practice this as often as you feel is necessary. Repetition increases its effectiveness.

Mindfully clearing your throat chakra provides the validation of self, which you may be sorely in need of. You are important, and what you say is important too. As you validate your voice, your aura glows more vibrantly.

Challenge Your People-Pleasing Aura · · · · · · · ·

It's easier to say what you know others want to hear when you have an empath aura. Blue, indigo, turquoise, and purple auras can sense what the people around them want to hear rather than what they may need to hear. Depending on childhood and societal programming, people-pleasing can become a huge issue in communication for any aura color. The turquoise aura who feels everyone's feelings so deeply can become stuck in repeating what they know others want to hear to feel loved and accepted. A purple aura may blurt out truths all the time only to find that it's not much appreciated, and then avoid these types of conversations altogether.

TAKING ACTION

1. Think about a time in your life when you felt you were stuck in a people-pleaser role. What did you feel when you were around others' energies?
2. Consider how your answer to step one relates to your aura and why.
3. Mindfully think of ways you can use this newfound knowledge to your advantage in similar situations moving forward. How can you make sure your ability to feel others' feelings isn't impeding your own necessary words and actions?

Understanding that speaking the truth (gracefully) is healing and not cruel is a lesson people-pleasing auras need to learn. The feelings you feel aren't always your own, and therefore, it isn't always your responsibility to modify your behavior to protect them.

Notice Nonverbal Auric Cues ·········

Communication isn't just about what is said; it's also about what isn't said. Depending on aura colors, a person can subconsciously show their energy through these cues via body language, how they seem to engage or retreat, and their ability to create or distract focus around themselves. The indigo aura who noticeably shrinks into the background of a group conversation or the orange aura who begins to wildly move their hands as they speak are examples of promoting the energy they are holding in the moment. The less clear or intentional attitudes they have toward the subject at hand may not be depicted in words but rather in the ways their energy is worn on their bodies.

TAKING ACTION

1. In a group setting, notice the unspoken cues of the people around you. Taking on an observational role, see how their words do or do not match up with what is being conveyed by their body language.
2. Consider the ways you see each aura color respond differently to energy in the conversation.
3. Reflect upon your ability to align your nonverbal cues with your authentic energy. In what ways can you mindfully improve it moving forward? For example, could you sit more authoritatively when you convey an emotion or uncross your arms when you are asserting yourself?

Picking up on nonverbal cues while communicating can create multi-layered insight into exchanges. Giving yourself an auric lens into how you and others subconsciously relay your energy can assist you in encouraging others to speak their truth or see how people *really* feel about an idea that is circulating.

Check Your Delivery ·········

How you intend to communicate and how well that intention aligns with how your words are received is tied to the aura. Self-awareness is a great assistant in coordinating your messages with the energy you are both giving off and identifying in the recipient. When someone isn't as mindful of their delivery, they can be met with obstacles from the people on the receiving end. The red aura who is too abrupt with a request may be construed as disrespectful, demanding, and rude. The yellow aura who sends off a message of detailed instruction to others could be misinterpreted as bossy and condescending. Turquoise auras delivering an important message to someone may be completely ignored altogether. Having an honest understanding of how your energy typically comes off to others gives you a better idea of how to deliver what you need to say in ways that are far more palatable to the ones who need to receive it.

TAKING ACTION

1. Envision asking someone for something important: How would you frame that request?
2. Reflect on how what you just said reflects your auric energy.
3. Now consider the ways others could interpret your communication. Think about the positives and the negatives.
4. Identify ways you can improve your methods or adjust them to different receiving aura colors in order to strengthen the delivery of an important message. Perhaps you need to say something more concisely or forcibly.

Coordinating your words and body language with the energy of your intended recipient is about validating their auric perspective. Being in line with how others best hear you ensures that you're heard.

Change Your Aura Perspective · · · · · · · · ·

Different aura colors see things with different filters. Blue auras may see the world as a frightening place in which they must help as many people as they can, while pink auras might view it more as a playground of their own limitless imaginations. No perspective is wrong; it's just how we all view this reality with the various energetic filters we hold. Thinking from a different aura point of view can expose you to new interpretations. These perspectives can in turn enhance your ability to communicate with different people.

TAKING ACTION

1. Pick an aura color that isn't your own.
2. Consider how this aura color may view the world.
3. Identify the similarities and differences between this perspective and how you see things.
4. Ask yourself what the benefits are to seeing the world as the other aura color does. Perhaps you would notice where fun could be had in a seemingly mundane routine, like the pink aura. Or you might better appreciate the passion your red aura coworker brings to a project.
5. Reflect on what you can do to bring a little of that point of view into your authentic perspective of how you see things. How could you get a little organized à la yellow aura? How could you show your passion for something in a way that gets others excited about it, like red auras do so skillfully?

The world is a fascinating place, especially when experienced through the eyes of another. Seeing via a different energetic lens gives you a unique vantage point that can be truly life changing.

Dig Deeper Into
Miscommunication ·········

The words you want to say may come out wrong in the moment. So, as you work on your communication skills and align them with your authentic aura, it's necessary to give yourself grace. There may have been an instance of miscommunication in your life that you see now as simply a difference of auric perspectives. Taking a moment to reflect on past instances of miscommunication and how they relate to auric energies can assist you in healing and gaining a valuable lesson from what transpired. The orange aura who can see that others may perceive their ambition as taking advantage or the indigo aura who understands that their disappearance was seen as abandonment can explain themselves better with this energetic approach.

TAKING ACTION

1. Reflect on a time when your energy was interpreted in a negative way.
2. Think about what you would say to the other person (or people) now if you could. How could you better explain your intentions? Consider how they felt, and choose words that validate their emotions and feelings.
3. Connect the miscommunication to their aura color and how it may have tied into their interpretations of your words and actions.

When you know better, you can do better. Forgiving yourself is important as you reflect on times in your life when your energy was not as refined as it could have been in delivering the messages you needed it to.

CHAPTER 4

· · · · · · · · · · · ·

Auras and Family

You came into the world a being of light, perfectly whole and ready to experience this world with your unique energy signature. The ones who raised you and allowed you to explore that inherent energy—or didn't— are critical elements in understanding your relationship with your aura and growing more into your authentic self. These individuals, be they parents, siblings, or extended relatives, were and still are formative in how you view the world; their energies had a say in how you saw and processed things. At times, you may have looked at the world through their filter instead of your own. The difficult or positive relationships you have with family can even be found repeated throughout your life in other relationships. Seeing these impactful family dynamics through an auric lens can allow you to consider the energies that have made it challenging to embrace your authentic self up to this point. The ones who raised you most likely prioritized their own energetic perspective, often in an attempt to keep you safe or to give you tips for success. In this chapter, you will separate your energy from the energies of family members and gain a more complete view of yourself and those you love.

What Your Aura Says about You

Each aura values family and handles familial situations in a unique way.

· · · · · **RED** · · · · ·

For a red aura, family means protection. To them, the dynamic of a family should provide the ones within it a haven from the chaos they feel from the world outside. Red auras in family roles take on leadership as a means of protecting the ones they love. They tend to feel responsible for all the problems of the people in their family unit, and because of that, they can come down hard on the "correct protocol" for how they believe life should be viewed and approached. Red auras are big on logical approaches to life in particular, so themes like personal responsibility, taking accountability, and earning respect through hard work and manners are stressed in their actions and viewpoints. They can see outsiders as threats, and they have a healthy dose of skepticism toward new people entering their family world. They sometimes feel the need to vet new significant others or friends, and seem to want the final say on whether someone they love has made an acceptable choice or not. This, of course, can lead to some people wanting to argue their own, differing perspectives in the family. Red auras take some time to get used to new ideas, but when approached with logic and respect, they tend to allow for change to happen. Change in the family is healthy, necessary, and inevitable. The red aura must learn to let the people around them evolve and, in doing so, understand that it's not a personal slight against them.

····· BLUE ·····

In a family, the blue auras are the glue that holds everything together. They tend to pick up the role of mediator in any sort of internal crisis and strive for peace in all they do. Blue auras place value on the emotional state of the family unit. They are so concerned with the energetic balance of a family, they will work to prevent any issues from arising in the first place. Taking the time to send an extra invite to the family member who needs to be especially welcomed to a holiday dinner or making sure a sibling decides to get rid of the chip on their shoulder before the big family gathering are ways blue auras predict and solve problems before they've even had a chance to manifest. This can leave blue auras feeling especially fatigued. The blue aura needs to learn that letting others have confrontations and discuss their own problems to find a solution is necessary. While allowing others to figure it out for themselves may be uncomfortable, it is also important for the long-term health of the family. Blue auras don't always know their place in a family if they aren't the glue that holds it all together, but teaching others the value of getting along and the beauty of working toward family peace creates an even stronger family bond.

····· YELLOW ·····

Planning ahead isn't always something others find value in. Yellow auras take it upon themselves, then, to do the planning for everyone, whether they've been asked to or not. In their love for their family, they will take an inventory of what someone needs or should be doing, and initiate steps toward those goals. They may take over the retirement plan and investment strategies for one family member or gather and collect college applications for another. They see what someone needs and, without even thinking about it, seek it out for them. This can lead to family members not understanding how to plan their own futures or not taking care of their own lives. It can also lead yellow auras to get stuck in the future instead of living in the moment with the people they love. They push aside the emotions of the now for the satisfaction of a future well executed. Yellow auras must learn that understanding why they do this and choosing the best times to do it are important for keeping their own energy in check and having some fun in the moment. The yellow aura can feel like a taskmaster instead of a family member, and being able to let others in on their special planning processes—and giving them the chance to do it themselves—will help the yellow aura feel more like a part of things than the director of all.

····· PURPLE ·····

The family unit is naturally a structured one, filled with roles and expectations. Purple auras are inclined to rebel against such established frameworks. Thus, the purple auras are usually the ones who shake things up in a family. By calling out idiosyncrasies, pointing out differences, and bringing up things they know others would rather leave be, the purple aura likes to create a bit of upheaval to encourage self-awareness. Because purple auras enjoy such digging, they like to watch others do the same, as deep down they know it's always for the best. Purple auras in families will point out more programmed nuances too—the wounds they notice in loved ones and how those affect the family as a whole. Forcing families to see, validate, heal, and grow is not always a comfortable thing to do, and because of that, purple auras can be ridiculed and made to feel guilty about their direct honesty. They can feel like outcasts and as if they are perpetually wrong and don't fit in anywhere. The purple aura must learn that just because not everyone enjoys seeing the multiple perspectives they do, they are still worthy points to make. The ability to speak to what isn't working and figure out how to get it back on track is an essential one—one that builds a family back better than before when executed with support and love from all involved.

· · · · · GREEN · · · · ·

The perception the world has of the family unit is very clear to the green aura. They can see how their family stacks up in terms of appearances, opportunities, money, and possessions. They often measure their family's success based on these more tangible aspects rather than emotional health or wellness. Green auras can feel their role is to ensure that their family is a self-sufficient system, one that can stand any test the world brings to it. They find it important to know the correct ways to do anything and create solid logic to bolster their strong positions. They may be very clear about which schools children should attend, when it's a good idea to get a job, or what constitutes a well-rounded and intelligent individual. Green auras in the family can seem impossible to measure up to; they are able to go far and fast, and they consider it possible for anyone who has the right mindset and work ethic to do the same. Green auras look to the health of the family as a system out of their love and devotion, but they must learn that it's important to peek *inside* the system from time to time as well. Connecting emotionally with the loved ones who make up the family unit allows everyone to be seen and to feel less like cogs in a machine. Green auras will learn that doing this enhances the power of the family insurmountably.

· · · · · INDIGO · · · · ·

The indigo aura tends to be the heart of the family unit. They foster much of their value from the bonds they create with the people they love most. Indigo auras find comfort in family relationships and joy in exploring and strengthening these relationships in as many ways as they can. The indigo aura can understand intentions with ease and therefore can sometimes ignore words and actions in favor of what they know lies beneath them. While this fosters a sense of safety and comfort with their family members, it can also lead to the indigo aura tolerating harmful or thoughtless behavior. They may excuse an inconsiderate act knowing deep down what the person is going through, or they may decide to let careless words slide if they can sense a loved one is suffering. The indigo aura must learn that just because they can sense the inner wounds of the people they love, they aren't obligated to ignore the actions that try to cover them up. Indigo auras in families must work to be heard and to get the respect they deserve. In doing so, they are forcing the ones they cherish to deal with their own pain bodies and heal wounds, and find their reasons for doing so. The indigo aura will understand over time that their role is not to be the place where others put their pain.

· · · · · PINK · · · · ·

In most families, there are people who stand out for different reasons. Pink auras are noticeable for their rosy outlook, positive personalities, and the fantasies they love to create and often refuse to let go of. Sometimes in families, the ones who stand out get called out, and pink auras are used to this role. They can often be the butt of the joke at the dinner table or family gathering or the one everyone rolls their eyes at. Pink auras will generally refuse to stand up for themselves when this happens, as the pain it causes leads them to retreat further into their bubbles of protection. The pink aura is adept at seeing when others need to feel that same sense of escape that they know is essential, so they will endorse lots of memory-making events for the ones they love. They find connection with their family in special experiences where everyone loses themselves for a moment and simply has a lovely time together. The pink aura must learn that their role in the family is not to be the punchline but rather the inspirational light for everyone to look to in times of darkness. They should understand that it is in this light that the truest soul of everyone they love can shine authentically.

····· TURQUOISE ·····

Any family unit has its fair share of secrets, some known to everyone involved and some hidden beneath years of generational trauma. The turquoise aura in a family ends up taking on the responsibility of digging up these secrets and shining them in the faces of everyone they hold dear. For that reason, turquoise auras don't always have it easy in their family units. The secrets no one wants to deal with or be accountable for are often projected back on the person who brought them to everyone's attention. The turquoise aura can feel the wrath of others' inability to deal with the honesty needed to heal and evolve. Turquoise auras are sweet energies; they want people to see what they so clearly do. Living their own lives in a constant state of openness, they can have a hard time understanding why anyone wouldn't want to properly deal with something that seems so obvious. The talks about relationships gone awry, situations that could have been handled better, and long-term effects of what happened are not taboo for the turquoise aura but rather are wonderful conversation starters for getting the healing energy flowing. Turquoise auras must learn that their ability to show the path to energy restoration isn't always welcomed, but the ones who want to see it will benefit greatly, and for that, the turquoise aura's work is important.

····· ORANGE ·····

Some families have a mission: a path they know they are destined to journey upon. The orange aura finds their role as the trailblazer of this quest, and they find much purpose in being called to whatever pursuit they undertake. The family business that hopes to be the best in the region or the family name that holds influence and prestige are undertakings an orange aura is passionate about. Orange auras are comfortable being the family member who pulls rank, placing themselves front and center as the focal point of the job at hand. They also have no problem delegating tasks to those around them while they take on the role of answering the questions and getting the credit. Orange auras do not mind being in the limelight, in fact, and feel their responsibility to the family increases their own mystique and allure to gain access to new places and opportunities. The orange aura must learn that some family members may resent them for taking all the credit for a job well done. They will find that the true way to blaze a path is by sharing both the accomplishments and the credit with all, which will create more trailblazers in the generations to come.

embracing your aura

Make Amends · · · · · · · · ·

In your family, there is probably at least one person you don't get along with. Your aura can trigger other people for different reasons. Perhaps your yellow aura mother with her organized ideas of how to run a household interpreted your purple aura inability to fold clothing as a personal slight. Or your strong and tough red aura dad often chided your blue aura for the many emotions you displayed. Exploring who aggravated you the most will reveal to you the places where you need to infuse a little empowerment today.

TAKING ACTION

1. Ask yourself, "Who is one family member I feel or felt the most at odds with?"
2. Analyze what you feel this family member's aura color is and how this created their life perspective.
3. Reflect on the ways this person caused you to feel animosity and how that still affects you today.
4. List all the things you feel they had or still have issues with that are parts of you. How do all those things relate to your aura?
5. Reflect upon their perspective with empathy.
6. Consider how you can take steps to feel more loud and empowered in the spaces you were silenced. If this person is in a good place with you, making a coffee date to reconnect may be mutually healing. If this feels impossible, you can write a letter to your past self as a way to reflect on your growth and journey.

Regardless of what the consistent conflicts may be, reflecting on them can reveal to you the ways you pushed yourself away aurically, as well as the parts of your aura you decided to show instead.

Nurture an Aura ·········

Parenting is not an easy job. It requires every part of you to participate, including your aura. The energy you live in and express is felt by your child. They know you better than anyone else because of the unconditional loving bond you share. Children can immediately sense your strengths and vulnerabilities and, without judgment, want to explore them. It's very normal that you will be tested energetically by your child, as they see you without any of the barriers you may subconsciously construct around the parts of yourself you don't feel comfortable expressing. If you are a blue aura parent, perhaps your child can upset your sense of family peace when they talk back, or, if you're a pink aura parent, your child might decide they are done with birthday parties this year, and you feel crushed. Children know your true energy, and the child who tests that is asking you to know it better yourself and develop it further.

TAKING ACTION

1. If you are a parent, mindfully reflect upon what you find easy about it and what you find difficult. If you are not a parent, reflect upon how your nurturing self shows up for family, friends, and even pets.
2. Consider how your answers in step one reflect your aura colors.
3. If you are a parent, note a few things that you feel have been revealed to you about yourself through parenting.

Your children are a portal back into your own inner child. Through them, you can see the energetic components you need help with and the ones that already shine. That which feels unsteady can be revealed to you quite plainly through the parent-child relationship.

Investigate Family Roles ·········

In every family, there is a potpourri of personalities that make up their own special mix of both chaos and love. Because of this, there is a need for defined roles to be formed. Subconsciously, family systems tend to task different members with their own category of utility. Your aura colors play into the jobs you were assigned early on in your family. Perhaps you were the calm-in-a-crisis yellow aura who is now the only one hosting any holiday gathering. Or you could be the informal family therapist, as the indigo aura no doubt understands. This activity will give you much-needed perspective on your role in your family system and help you understand how to connect more to the family dynamics you want and let go of what doesn't serve you anymore.

TAKING ACTION

1. Think about what your role has been in your family. Consider patterns, specific incidents, and how you were asked to do certain tasks.
2. Reflect upon how this role makes you feel. Is this a good feeling for you or just what you are "supposed" to do?
3. Now think about how this role you were given plays out in other relationships in your life. How does it impact your actions and reactions at work? With friends? In relationships?
4. Reflect on how this role relates to your aura colors. Is this a natural role for you? What parts of your aura are/were being taken advantage of or not used enough?

The key part of understanding your role in the family is seeing how it affects your self-worth, your subconscious thoughts, and your attitude surrounding how you feel you give worth to the world around you.

Host an Aura Game Night ·········

There is no better way to spend quality time with the unique energies in your family than by having a good old-fashioned game night. The togetherness of the event and the simple joy of playing a game bring out everyone's authentic colors. Seeing the energy of the people in your family come out and participate will leave you with some interesting insights to carry into your relationships. You may watch the orange aura do anything to win at Monopoly or see the purple aura win big at Pictionary. The possibilities are endless, and the amount of fun you can all have together while spending time with your truest energies will make your bonds stronger.

TAKING ACTION

1. Plan a game night with a few options for what games you will play.
2. As you see everyone interact during the night, make mental notes of the auras at work.
3. Consider how your own aura comes out in these fun contexts.
4. After the game night, reflect on how you feel closer to the people in your life simply by spending some quality time together in this way.

Being with family in this context creates a strong family unit. It's a safe place for family members to share their true selves and know that they can be accepted, loved, and seen for who they really are. Intense conversations are good to have, but every once in a while, having some simple fun is the most profound bonding activity of all.

Have Fun with Furry Family Members ·········

Pets are family too, and the animals in your life are soulful companions who know you very well. Just like people, animals communicate with energy—often more so than other forms of communication. With mindful observation, you can uncover how you interact with your pet and how it relates to your own aura. You could be a nonverbal energy communication expert like a lot of green auras are, making sure your dog walks well-behaved on a leash. Or you could be the indigo aura who allows your cats to sleep on you at night and wake you up at their preferred breakfast hour. Your aura is what your animals know best, and they react to it accordingly. Taking some time to observe how you interact and what that says about you can assist you with not only knowing yourself a bit better but also improving your animal-human relationships.

TAKING ACTION

1. Think about a pet in your life, past or present, and reflect on your relationship with this animal.
2. Consider how this relationship and your interactions with this pet relate to your aura.
3. In what ways did your pet know your true self? How could you tell?

Your furry soulmates are energetic beings who, no matter what you think or say, listen to your authentic aura to communicate with you. They can assist you in exploring the frequencies you give off in a more reflective way.

Take a Step Back ·········

In the spirit of wanting everyone in a family to get along and move forward at their highest potential, you can easily find yourself in the middle of an issue that doesn't involve you. You may have been so effective at being a mediator or problem-solver that people don't seem to know what to do without your intervention. Your aura is usually evident in the ways this situation presents itself. Perhaps you are the blue aura who decides to buffer a miscommunication between two other family members. Or you could be the purple aura who hears the gossip that isn't helpful. Noticing when you're in the middle of a family conflict that doesn't concern you and stepping back so those involved can solve their own issues is imperative to your energetic health and the strength of the family itself.

TAKING ACTION

1. Reflect upon a time that you were in the middle of a problem that wasn't your own. What was your role?
2. Identify how this situation and the role you assumed relates to your aura.
3. Now think about how your involvement caused you stress and fatigue.
4. Consider alternatives to getting involved in the same way the next time a similar situation arises. Set the intention to allow family members to resolve their conflicts on their own.

While it's normal to want to smooth things over in families, it's not always a good thing to be involved. Understanding where you can take a step back allows others to deal with what they need to on their own and enables you to place your energy in more useful contexts.

Create Boundaries ·········

Nothing tests the limits of your comfort level more than your family unit, and the people who know you the best can use that to their advantage. Whether they mean to or not, families can push your buttons and make self-advocating very stressful. Your aura can have a role in what boundaries you may need and in why it can be hard to create those boundaries. The red aura who has to stop lending money to the family member who keeps asking for it struggles with their feeling of failure in protecting others. The indigo aura who needs to set some limits with a family member they've been enabling can feel as if they are turning their back on a loved one's pain. Creating boundaries is difficult but necessary—not only for your own health but for the health of the family as well.

TAKING ACTION

1. Reflect on something family members may do that makes you uncomfortable.
2. Consider how this discomfort relates to your aura.
3. Mindfully think about why you fear creating a boundary to avoid this discomfort in the future.
4. Make a mental note of the boundary that would target this discomfort, and picture a life where this boundary is not crossed. In your visualization of life with this boundary, do you feel better? How so?

Thinking about what personal boundaries are needed with your family, what has kept you from creating them in the past? Imagining how beneficial they would be can build the motivation to establish those boundaries now and get the family unit back on track—even if not everyone will see it as a good thing at first.

Accept Their Aura · · · · · · · ·

It takes an abundance of diverse energies to create a successful and loving family. Accepting others for who they are isn't just about being kind; it's also about validating their authentic selves. It can be difficult in a family to feel like an outcast for being different, and depending on familial programming, certain aura colors can experience this feeling, like the sensitive blue aura boy who doesn't fit his competitive red aura father's idea of what a man should be or the idealistic pink aura child who is told that their escapism and creative fantasy play is nonsense and useless. Thinking about where you weren't accepted in your family can assist you in making space for others to never feel the same way.

TAKING ACTION

1. Reflect on a time when you felt different from the rest of your family. Contemplate the people who made you feel this way and the circumstances surrounding this time in your life.
2. Consider how your aura created this different feeling for you.
3. Now think about ways you can create a safe feeling for the people in your family today to feel accepted as they are.

Family is where we need to feel accepted, loved, and given space to be exactly who we are. Making sure our own insecurities, triggers, and limitations don't get in the way of each other's need to evolve and grow energetically is essential for creating a secure and stable family system.

CHAPTER 5

• • • • • • • • • • •

Auras and Mental Health and Well-Being

How you've been able to cope with all you have gone through in life takes on a powerful new perspective when viewed through the lens of your aura. You have successfully navigated your way here today, and regardless of how well you think you did, the universe sees your course as brilliant. You have consciously come to this very moment ready to see yourself authentically and take the next steps to level up your energy. Part of that journey is understanding that you aren't here to just survive life but to thrive in every way possible. Instead of criticizing your past mistakes or feeling weighed down by traumas, you can approach the world anew through the scope of your auric energy. The things you may have thought were weaknesses could actually be untapped auric superpowers. The insecurities that held you back from embracing who you are can be worked with rather than ignored. The rest you need to restore your mind can be claimed. There is power in you; it's simply waiting to be seen for what it is and celebrated instead of being shrugged off or compartmentalized. In this chapter, you'll be able to turn what you may have previously labeled as faults and imperfections into tools for wellness and personal growth.

What Your Aura Says about You

Each aura has unique needs for nurturing their mental health and well-being.

· · · · · RED · · · · ·

Red auras enjoy being in control, and at those times when control is taken away in life, they react with extreme emotion. Without the self-awareness needed to understand the true underlying causes of their heightened feelings, they can instead find ways to react that drive others away. They may unhealthily demonstrate their rage or attempt to control other environments that don't suit them. Red auras can be very insecure about their ability to lead, and when they don't feel they are at a place in life that has an appreciative climate to do so, they will take it as a deep-seated failure of their character. Red auras can become fixated on a point, ranting and raving unnecessarily in a situation that requires logic and justice—especially when feeling they are not heard. When imbalanced, red auras can be perceived as high-risk friends or partners, angry, or caustic. They can see any offer of assistance as an insult, and any critique feels like rubbing salt in their already sore ego wounds. Deep down, they will reject the love and acceptance they don't feel they deserve because of their inability to create what they desire—that is, places for people to be protected and heard. A mindful red aura understands that control is something that must be first enacted within. Finding ways to create this feeling in themselves is a healthy first step in replicating it in their outside environments.

· · · · · BLUE · · · · ·

Blue auras enjoy being needed and will find places in their lives and relationships to act out this desire. The true motivation of the blue aura is to receive a feeling of light from the person they assist—a feeling that they are connecting with something greater than all of us, the need to be seen and unconditionally loved as is. When a blue aura believes they've found this feeling in another, they receive their energetic compensation. A blue aura who is imbalanced, however, may notice that their intrinsic need to help others is not always reciprocated. Sometimes, blue auras who are in this unaware state seek out people and environments that purposely shut them out, devalue them, or make them feel invisible. As a result, the blue aura may begin to feel victimized, stuck in a never-ending cycle of give, give, give without a way out. They outsource their joy and satisfaction only to benefit others' feelings, always needing more to feed their own self-worth. An awakened blue aura will understand that the love you give to others doesn't always have to be expressly acknowledged or returned, but it does have to be put in places where, in some way, that feeling of light will carry on. Giving to the right people creates the right feelings for the blue aura to continue their compassionate pursuits.

· · · · · YELLOW · · · · ·

The ability to catch a flaw and fix it is the yellow aura's specialty. This perceptive skill, however, can be turned inward to their own self-talk and subconscious self-beliefs. Since yellow auras are naturally driven toward states of perfection, they can be unnecessarily self-critical. Yellow auras have an eye for detail, not only in their environments but also in their own processes, bodies, and personal choices, making it almost impossible to ignore or postpone self-improvement. While yellow auras take on projects that most people find daunting and tedious, they can have a harder time turning that approach inward. A person's own mindsets, traumas, and healing are not as easy to fix as organizing a pantry or balancing a checkbook, as they take appropriate time and evolve at their own pace. Yellow auras are notoriously impatient, and instead of giving due grace to their own timelines for healing and growth, they attempt to speed things up with caustic self-talk. Since they are often seen as inordinately capable beings, they also aren't given the emotional checks others seem to give one another. This can reinforce the negative inner dialogue and belief that they are supposed to be stronger, faster, and more durable than anyone else. The yellow aura must give themselves over to self-care and see it as a wonderful process that moves at its own pace. The mental wellness journey itself dictates what it needs as it goes along, and the yellow aura will learn to find comfort in its unique timeline.

····· PURPLE ·····

When the purple aura desires an adjustment to their reality and cannot seem to get it in ways comfortable to them, they may plant seeds of destruction instead. Purple auras love to change it up as they evolve within their dynamic environments. Yet it is difficult to do this, as the world can see it as flaky or flippant behavior, erratic, and irresponsible. This leaves the purple aura still wanting change but feeling undeserving of it and ashamed of this need. When the unaware purple aura doesn't understand this obstacle, they take matters into their own hands. Subconsciously setting up places in which to destroy parts of their life is an almost hypnotic go-to activity. They can create drama in the job they don't feel they can leave, hoping instead to get fired. Or they become dishonest in a relationship they feel bad about ending themselves, hoping the other person breaks it off first. The way in which the purple aura leaves something is a direct reflection of the punishment they feel they deserve for wanting something new—for craving a change they so desperately and energetically need. An awakened purple aura understands that the mistakes of the past were the result of a lack of self-awareness and that their goal for the future should be to confront head-on the stigma society has for the choices that best suit them.

· · · · · GREEN · · · · ·

Green auras see everything at once from a bird's-eye view. The way things work, what the continued trajectories are, and what systems are defunct are obvious to them. Because of this, they can have a hard time coming back down to the places where the rest of the world seems to reside. They avoid conflict, drama, and inane back-and-forth with others that don't fit into the bigger picture they so happily enjoy concentrating on. Green auras need to stay in a space where they feel they are creating better systems for the world to utilize. Either in big or little ways, improving something is the green aura's path to peace. Unaware green auras who feel deprived of this can become cold, numb, and detached. Their logic, which is best used in challenging projects, can turn on itself. They can start creating reasons as to why they are stuck the way they are and why they will not be able to rise back into the places they enjoy being. Accused of being cold, angry, or empty, green auras can learn to stay that way since it can feel better than confronting any ill-conceived logic. Conversely, the aware green aura will find the ways they can enact their true visionary selves in new areas of their life, no matter how inconsequential or unnecessary these changes may first appear to be. They will find their way again to the places they know they want to go.

· · · · · INDIGO · · · · ·

There is great beauty in this world, along with great sadness. Indigo auras are able to feel both, not just through themselves but also through the energy of everyone they encounter. This ability to feel others' feelings and to feel the way their own feelings make others feel is overwhelming to the unbalanced indigo aura. Indigo auras love to connect with others, rummage through their pain bodies, and light paths for them to begin a journey of healing. That said, when they aren't respectful of their own energy, they can become burned out more quickly than most. They begin to feel overstimulated and set off by the slightest of environmental sounds, bright lights, and especially societal pressure put upon them. Society will often label this behavior as lazy, incapable, or slow. Unaware indigos may start to believe this too, eventually creating a sense of failure within their own psyches. When the indigo aura is aware that this ability is something that must be respected, they understand that the depth at which they can travel with one person is just as worthy as what another may be able to do at a surface level with many more. Quality is their goal, not quantity. They must recognize that their sensitive energies require isolated time away to rebuild the strength to continue their healing work in a way that is replenishable and resourceful.

····· PINK ·····

Finding joy in the little things tends to get more difficult as one ages. We are born with a natural capacity to see it, merge with it, and be present all the while. But from a young age, we are taught to move along from such heartening moments and focus instead on the unseen duties lying ahead. Against all odds, pink auras somehow retain this natural ability to find joy as they mature, and because they are able to do that, they end up being fiercely protective of it. When faced with struggle, conflict, and turmoil, they jump into their auric force field, shutting out anything—good or bad—that approaches them. Pink auras are often told they are incapable, untrustworthy, and silly. The unaware pink aura, over a lifetime of these messages, can begin to believe it. They internalize the message that the world isn't meant for them—that they must sit back and allow others to take over instead. The aware pink aura, meanwhile, confronts this attitude knowing that they are strong enough to both find their joy *and* live successfully. They see that the ridicule of others comes from a painful wound within them; it is not a wound that must be shared by their own pink glow. Awakened pink auras understand that if you can find joy in the here and now, you are the most powerful person in the universe.

····· TURQUOISE ·····

For a turquoise aura, the idea of being in the moment takes on a whole new meaning. Unable to separate themselves from the contexts they find themselves in, they have a harder time than most deciphering who they really are. Their identity, preferences, goals, and dreams become enmeshed with the environmental vibrations, leaving them to wonder what it is that makes them unique. The unaware turquoise can be picked on often for this by others, called out as being a follower or as someone who says things without the awareness needed to fit in. As life's struggles unfold, they can feel helpless as they float along without attaching any intuitive pull as to which direction to go. The aware turquoise understands they have more sovereignty than they realize. They know that the ability to enmesh with the life-force energies all around is their most powerful gift and that reflecting these energies back to the ones who need to experience them is their life path. The turquoise aura is naturally adventurous, and they find their identity is being able to hover above what society calls "identity" and relish in their citizenship with energy itself.

····· ORANGE ·····

There is a prize to be won in life, and the aware orange aura sees it clearly. The obstacles they find in their way are delightful puzzles they get to solve. Orange auras burn through challenges others find too hard to endure, and, in doing so, they can be ridiculed by many who feel incapable. Orange auras tie their self-worth to their drive, needing to up their game in every space they show up in. The unaware orange aura, however, can avoid these pursuits as they buy into the more popular perception that what they want is unattainable. Orange auras who stop their force from pushing ahead can feel stifled and upset. They can isolate and prefer the company of people who tell them what they want to hear instead of what is real. They can become irritable and upset at any reminder that they aren't at the epicenter of the revolutionary change they so intuitively seek. Little inconveniences can set them off as they begin to seek smaller and smaller contexts in which to retreat. The aware orange aura knows that success is not defined by getting what you want but by the act of going after it at all. In a world where so many stop themselves out of fear of failure, the aware orange aura takes initiative.

embracing
your aura

Confront Your Aura ·········

The way you react to confrontation can tell you a lot about the best way to interact with your authentic energy. Perhaps as a red aura, you expect confrontation with all you do, and you feel somewhat confused when you aren't met with it. It's possible that as an indigo aura, you feel paralyzed when met with confrontation and look for a way to disappear. The stressful interactions between yourself and others cause knee-jerk reactions that can illuminate who you are and what other traumas and triggers have shaped you.

TAKING ACTION

1. Think about the last time you had any sort of confrontation.
2. Focus on your emotional state at that time. How did you feel? Did you experience any physical feelings? What did you feel afterward? How does it feel right now to recount this experience?
3. Reflect upon how the feelings that came up tie into your past experiences. Did this remind you of something from when you were growing up? Is this a reminder of a specific incident that impacted you?
4. Think about how your aura plays into this confrontation reaction.
5. Choose a trusted friend to role-play the situation you have recounted. Use new words and be intentional in your delivery. As you do so, notice how you are better able to deal with confrontation following the reflection you've done.

Your go-to move in these uncomfortable situations, as well as how you either avoid or expect them, can cue you into a lot more than how you deal with them. It can reveal to you some internal blockages between you and your authentic energy.

Find Aura Pet Peeves ·········

We all have that one thing (or multiple things) that can really fire us up and create a sensation of pure anger. For a yellow aura, it could be a larger theme such as inconsiderate behavior, or it might be a smaller nuance such as a negative comment from someone that the orange aura finds pessimistic. The things you focus on with emotional intensity, such as pet peeves, can demonstrate a subtle, more energetic component worth paying attention to. Your pet peeves can be little triggers, and experiencing them can feel like the world is pushing a button that activates a deep inner wound left unresolved. A red aura seeing someone not using their turn signal may feel deep rage at people who don't follow basic safety rules. It could trigger a deep-seated wound from a time when they didn't feel safe or cared for. Little things can often spark deep self-revelation.

TAKING ACTION

1. Reflect on one of your pet peeves. Consider all the emotions that come with thinking about it.
2. Ask yourself why you think this triggers you more than other people.
3. Connect your pet peeve to your aura. How does this pet peeve and the reasons behind it line up with your authentic energy?

Understanding what your pet peeves reveal about you emotionally and energetically may be the catalyst you need to up the authentic ante in your life.

Discover Your Inner Child Aura ·········

The you who exists now is a mix of your authentic self and the ways you have had to mold yourself to fit your surroundings. Parents and caregivers, society, and generational trauma all leave an imprint on your energy signature. Children are born new and free of this molding. For a time, they resist the intrusive outside energies that tear at their inherent authenticity. Perhaps you loved to study bugs and play alone, as a green aura child would. Or maybe you were a precocious performer, creating theatrical plays for others to watch, as a purple aura child may have done. Thinking of yourself through the lens of your inner child mindset can reveal to you some things left behind that may be worth picking up again.

TAKING ACTION

1. Reflect on yourself as a child. You may wish to look at a picture of your younger self as you do, or, if memory is not serving you, ask trusted family members some questions about what you were like as a child.

2. Mindfully reminisce about your favorite games, toys, friends, and dreams. What did you enjoy doing as a child? Why? Can you remember the feelings you associated with these experiences?

3. Consider how the things you enjoyed as a child showcase your authentic self. In what ways does it call back your aura colors?

4. Hang up a picture of yourself as a child in a place you'll see regularly. When you look at this picture, reflect on who you are within.

Being changed by this world is part of everyone's journey, and seeing how it happened is part of healing and growing as you deserve.

Redefine You ·········

The thoughts you have about yourself may not be exactly true. Perhaps as a yellow aura, you were told how capable you were as a child, leaving your adult self confused as to how to ask for and receive assistance. Or maybe throughout your whole life as a pink aura, you were told what a foolish scatterbrain you were, and now you feel incapable of meeting others' expectations. Investigating all of the definitions of yourself that you have internalized over the years can be a vulnerable and sensitive endeavor. It may feel tough at first, as we tend to bury these beliefs deep into places where they feel like actual truth. Nevertheless, as you do this, you can change the way you are perceived not only by yourself but by the world around you.

TAKING ACTION

1. Thinking about your aura colors, identify some ways in which you feel aligned with them that may not always be positive.
2. Ponder the ways you find this definition of you to be true. In what ways is it not true?
3. Consider how this "agreement" of who you are has been perpetuated by others, and now yourself, over the course of your life.
4. Brainstorm ways you can make changes so as to break the false narrative you have about yourself. Think about what kind of language you can use to describe yourself and how you can incorporate new activities, styles, or experiences you may have previously dismissed based on what you were told.

Breaking agreements you've made about yourself is equivalent to breaking the chains that are holding you back from living your truest version of life. Through the lens of the aura, this work can become a bit more streamlined.

Look Within Instead of Beyond · · · · · · · ·

Throughout your life, there have likely been times when you outsourced your happiness. You created a conditional relationship to it based on the feelings and judgments of others instead of your own, and in doing so, you lost your ability to find happiness within. Fortunately, your aura can give you a direction to go to find that joy. Perhaps as a turquoise aura, you have an innate love for healing modalities, or as an orange aura, you crave expansive projects to tackle. Finding your happy space is about finding yourself and creating a place to express your energy authentically. When you find your joy, you revitalize your inner world and reset emotions that have been weighing you down. Don't worry about starting small: Finding your joy is like taking care of a little plant, knowing in time it will grow.

TAKING ACTION

1. Ponder your aura colors: Where are the general places that they seem to point the ways to finding joy and comfort?
2. Consider whether there are any activities you have done or currently do that align with your aura.
3. Think of a few joyful activities you can begin to do regularly, and do one now.
4. Afterward, ask yourself what you felt before, during, and after the activity.

Part of creating complete energetic well-being is to find a place to nurture your joy. Through understanding your aura, the search for joy becomes clearer and isn't outsourced to other people's ideas of what happiness should look like.

Learn to Cope ·········

When the world pushes on you with stress, change, or unexpected situations, it can feel suffocating. The trick to dealing with this is to create an energetic peace within you, one that the outside world can't affect, no matter how hard it tries. Coping techniques come with practice and an inherent, mindful understanding of one's own energetic makeup. As a red aura, you may find yourself in a zen space when you concentrate on lifting weights. As a green aura, you may notice that throwing yourself into the care of your lawn calms your mind. And a blue aura may find that meditation practices have long-lasting effects. Your coping strategies will be guided by your aura colors, and following the lead of your authentic energy will lay the path to inner wellness.

TAKING ACTION

1. List healthy activities that help you feel calm.
2. Envision a time when you were coping successfully with a stressful situation. How did you manage?
3. Consider how the activities and coping strategies you identified in steps one and two relate to your aura.
4. Reflect on ways you can weave these coping techniques into your everyday life.
5. Commit to implementing one healthy activity every day this week that serves your authentic aura.

Knowing your aura gives you the blueprint for building not only that peaceful oasis inside of you but also strategies to deal with all challenges in life.

Change Your Mind ·········

In some way or another, you were taught and conditioned not to listen to your authentic energies. The parts of you that pull and push your motivations can be shut out with practice, programming, and a side of fear. It can be tempting to be the person others would wish you to be. Over time, you can build a life based on fear rather than who you really are. Eventually, though, your aura will give you messages that something is not right—that a change is needed. The red aura may suddenly realize that working for a company isn't as rewarding as starting their own. The blue aura may feel the need to end a friendship that is harmful. It's okay to change your mind, and the more familiar you are with your innate auric energy, the easier it will be to know what choice to make in the first place.

TAKING ACTION

1. Think about the things in your life you aren't exactly satisfied with. Why aren't you satisfied? What would you prefer instead?
2. Consider how your answers in step one reflect your aura.
3. The next time you need to make a choice today, practice this reflection. If your friend asks for a favor, ask yourself whether you want to do that favor or whether you should keep that commitment you signed up for earlier this week.
4. Get in the habit of practicing this before making any choices for a few days.
5. Make one change this week based on your reflections.

When you listen to yourself, the changes you make start in your mind, rewiring how you think about a decision, from "What should I do?" to "What is authentic to me and my desires?" When it is time to act, the world doesn't seem as fearsome as it did before.

Make Fifteen Minutes for You ·········

The world wants your time, to eat it up and tell you there is none left over for you. Society's message is to find any time you have left and to spend it in places that serve others, not yourself. But making time for your own well-being is important. It is what keeps your energy flowing and vibrant. And you can discover how to do this by using your own energy imprint. The yellow aura can begin a calligraphy class online during their lunch hour. The green aura can tend to their herb garden on the windowsill at their office. Making time for you to be you tells the universe to send along more contexts that serve your authentic energy.

TAKING ACTION

1. Think of when in your day you could take fifteen minutes just for yourself.
2. Ponder some activities, no matter how small, that reflect a genuine interest you have.
3. Consider how these activities and this interest relate to your aura.
4. Choose one activity and spend fifteen minutes working on it today.
5. Celebrate your achievement with some positive self-talk about how this activity has allowed you to express your true self.

No matter how short this activity is, the impact will be life altering. The time you invest in yourself is the time best spent. It lets the frequencies of the universe align with you and respond to your attention. By doing this, you'll find even more places to feel authentically invested in your wellness.

CHAPTER 6

· · · · · · · · · · · ·

Auras and Physical Health

The auric energy around you is your spiritual body, and the relationship it has with your physical body is a symbiotic one; when one body suffers, the other will too. Understanding your energetic needs creates a feeling of peace and calm that permeates your physical, spiritual, and mental well-being. Your aura will speak to you through physical symptoms when it's crying out for attention, and each aura color tends to have its own language for doing so. The person who is not speaking their truth may develop tooth problems. The person who is not dealing with planning for the future may suffer foot issues due to their fear of moving ahead in life. The medicine for many of these kinds of ailments are not ones you can find in a pharmacy; rather, you will find them in practicing physical self-care and reflecting on the deeper source of your symptoms. This chapter will explore the aura's unique way of letting you know something is imbalanced in your energetic body by way of your physical one. You will better learn how to hear the cries for attention and how to answer them with practices that benefit both your energy and your physical health.

What Your Aura Says about You

Each aura has unique needs for cultivating and maintaining physical health and promoting energetic flow.

· · · · · RED · · · · ·

The strong energy of the red aura is one that enjoys feeling the push of the world upon them. They look for places to expend their excess drive and create movement where there seemingly is none. They are always running a little hot, ready at any moment to jump into action. Red auras look for adrenaline; they seek out the fire that motivates them into action. However, when they aren't feeling as in control as they would like to in their environments, their physical bodies can begin to pay the toll, as they attempt to create that fire in other ways. Red auras must be watchful of cardiac issues, high blood pressure, and a tendency to take unnecessary risks with their physical well-being. They pride themselves on going hard and fast and stopping when they feel they want to. This can lead to binge activities with substances. Red auras can often follow their energetic ailments down to a feeling of restriction somewhere in their lives. Taking control of their body by weight lifting, cardio, or athletic challenges can assist them in feeling confident in themselves moving forward. Red auras who have physical symptoms not only need to seek medical care; they must also complete a thorough reflection of where they need more control in their life and what steps they can take to achieve that control for wellness.

· · · · · BLUE · · · · ·

The blue aura has a mission to be needed, and so, they can muffle the cries of help their body elicits. The problem is not that they are able to empathically pick up on these outside energies but that they prioritize them over their own. When this happens, as it so often does for the blue aura, the health of the physical body can suffer. Silent multi-symptomatic warning bells go off in their bodies; hormonal fluctuations, autoimmune disorders, and other long-term syndromes can manifest within the blue aura's physical self as a cry for attention. While seeking medical advice is always recommended, it's most helpful when the blue aura understands it's not just a physical condition but an energetic one as well. Learning what they have been ignoring in themselves and finding ways to listen and prioritize their own voice is imperative in recovery. Blue auras can regain this voice by way of meditation and contemplative physical activities such as nature walking or connecting with animals. Knowing that they are actually more helpful to the ones they love when they are at their healthiest is a motivating factor for a blue aura to practice physical self-care. Blue auras would prefer to live in a quiet, invisible state so as not to be a bother to the ones they love. However, in doing so, they can fail to realize that taking care of oneself is the best way to be of assistance to others.

· · · · · YELLOW · · · · ·

Some things in life are difficult to swallow, and yellows understand that better than anyone. Yellow auras see the world as it is, plainly and honestly with little sugar coating. They seek out truths and prefer them delivered straight and in line with the facts. Since yellow auras never shy away from protecting themselves from all of life's revelations, critiques, and realizations, over time, they can become hypersensitive to processing them. Digestive problems and irritable bowel issues seem to afflict yellow auras. In an attempt to control their demeanor, their systems of internal regulation can speak up when they are feeling unheard. Yellow auras often struggle with infertility and other reproductive health sensitivities. This often reflects a need for more self-nurturing and inner child expression. Yellow auras have a hard time giving themselves the empathy and kindness they so deserve. The path to wellness for yellow auras, then, becomes more than paying attention to their physical body. Physical attention with intensified focus such as Pilates and yoga, purposeful reorganization of their time so as to free up their busy minds, and adding their own self-care to a daily schedule can assist with this. Feeling their feelings, taking time to step away from the harsh truths they seek out, and giving themselves grace so as to digest new information properly can help the yellow aura reach a more stable state of harmony within their physical well-being.

· · · · · PURPLE · · · · ·

Purple auras need new projects, people, and places that feel vibrant so they can express themselves. They urgently demand change and actively seek it out to grow. When life becomes stagnant, purple auras can experience pent-up energy that, while always present, seems to flow much more comfortably through them when life is on the move. When a purple aura is not expressing themselves in the spirited way they need to be, they can take that out on themselves, sometimes in self-destructive ways. Purple auras may struggle with addiction, disordered eating, and other self-harming practices. When they feel stuck in their lives, they try to fight and claw their way out of their own bodies, possibly by making their lives difficult with poor choices and harmful habits. Purple auras who aren't listening to their intuitive self may also suffer from eye ailments due to a lack of third eye practice or creative contexts. Frequent healthy yet spontaneous changes that give them that feeling of freedom are helpful to the purple aura's mind-body connection. Purple auras are complex creatures who, on their journey to a well body, need to honor and respect the importance of creative outlets, exciting prospects, and expressed analysis so as to feel balanced, heard, and healthy.

· · · · · GREEN · · · · ·

In the green aura's life, systematic approaches are prioritized over anything else. They pride themselves on efficiency and an overall vision of peaceful inner workings. Loose ends are dealt with or ignored when they don't fit the preferred perception. Emotions and thoughts that interfere with the green aura's predetermined best route moving forward can become backed up over time, causing the body to speak out. Green auras may often experience ligament and joint pain, as the fear of moving forward in life manifests in their physical self. Green auras also tend to suffer from allergies and other lung and respiratory issues, as if the act of breathing itself is how their energy reminds them that one must filter their thoughts and emotions. Green auras thrive in natural surroundings that challenge their physical endurance. Leveling up their weekend hike, signing up for the next marathon, or even committing themselves to make the backyard the garden of their dreams are all ways in which they can care for their health. On the path to wellness, green auras must learn to consider the various things they so effortlessly compartmentalize in order to feel the flow of life move through them once again. The body of the green aura will stop for them to take a closer look, halting their ever-persistent need to produce and innovate and thus creating space for the energetic self to unbox and make its voice heard too.

· · · · · INDIGO · · · · ·

Being seen is a stressful event for an indigo aura. Because of their heightened ability to feel others' feelings, pain bodies, and unspoken emotions, they tend to stay well below the radar of others to avoid triggering them. The sensation of being watched, or paid attention to, can be energetically inundating. When an indigo aura experiences the energies of others, they feel responsible for fixing them, as well as feeling forced to repress their own needs to do so. The energetic overwhelm can be stifling. Indigos can take their invisibility to a new level when they are not self-reflecting on the innermost reasons for their social absence. Multi-symptomatic auto-immune issues, tooth pain, and throat pain can persist when the body is asking them to pay attention to these auric messages. The indigo aura tends to live in low lights, away from technology and the ever-persistent sounds of machines and bright spaces. Their physical sensitivity to the world around them can become unbearable when they need to give more awareness to their energetic sensitivity. Swimming is a very helpful activity to ease the stimulation they often feel, as are long meditation sessions and breathing-centered yoga practices. The body of an indigo aura appreciates the moments it can slow down and simply feel its own systems running through it instead of filtering an endless stream of others' systems.

· · · · · PINK · · · · ·

The worlds pink auras create to feel comfortable and fully themselves can also become prisons of their own design. When pink auras are constantly retreating into their joy bubbles to disassociate and distract themselves from problems that need their attention, their bodies can begin to do the reminding for them. Pink auras can find themselves out of practice with coping mechanisms for dealing with the difficult things life inevitably throws their way. In doing so, they can become disassociated from their physical bodies, which creates a false sense of self that replaces who they authentically are. While living their fantasy a little too vividly, they can ignore healthy eating, medical self-care, and other things that are a necessary if unexciting part of life. Pink auras can suffer from body dysmorphia, a feeling of disconnect with their internal systems, and hormonal issues as their bodies cry out for them to return to physical self-care rhythms and routines. Pink auras benefit greatly from therapy, nutrition counseling, and other down-to-earth yet nurturing self-help that can bring them back to their bodies. By avoiding filters, mirrors, and social media, they can begin to see themselves as they are instead of through a lens of subjective reality. Taking a dance class, joining up with a theater group, or simply enjoying some at-home fun workouts can reconnect them to the skin they are in.

····· TURQUOISE ·····

As a sort of energetic sponge for all the vibrations around them, the turquoise aura knows about holding things that are not their own. Their endlessly curious aura naturally seems to spend time with others, mingling and bringing back insightful tidbits of information that help them serve and heal. Their energetic overwhelm will become apparent in the physical body as they seemingly begin to deal with an onslaught of full body symptoms. Dermatological issues such as rashes, random food intolerances, and multi-symptomatic whole-body flare-ups are just some of the ailments that plague a turquoise aura who has reached their limit. Medical professionals can be at a loss for what the root causes are. These are energetic callbacks to the auric need to define oneself, listen, and validate what the turquoise aura needs to pay attention to within. A careful pairing of both medical treatment and spiritual insight can assist the turquoise aura back into a happy equilibrium. Seeing these body signals as indications to consult not only a doctor but also the energetic self as a whole becomes a lesson for the turquoise aura. There are limits the turquoise aura needs to learn about themselves, which will give a much-needed boundary to the energy that wanders off and accumulates borrowed vibes in their physical bodies when they fail to do so.

····· ORANGE ·····

The orange aura is a vibrant energy that rarely shows any sort of vulnerability in the physical form. Because of the orange aura's ability to focus and direct their energy, health issues can be at a minimum. They seem to understand how to self-manage their auric flow better than most. Orange auras have an enviable ability to prioritize their evolution and development so as to deter their physical bodies from intervening with symptomatic messages. Nevertheless, this changes when the orange aura hears the word "no" too often. When shut down and confronted with obstacles on the path forward, they can experience some telling health issues. Orange auras who are feeling repressed and shut down can experience obstructive symptoms in their intestinal and vascular health. Orange auras must therefore pay close attention to circulation and their digestive well-being. When life isn't moving at a breakneck speed, orange auras can feel stuck and uncomfortable, both in their spiritual bodies and their physical ones. Getting invested in friendly yet competitive athletic competitions with friends, beating their own record in a physical challenge, or learning a new and active game to play gives the orange aura the excitement and confidence they crave, with all the bodily benefits they need. The orange aura must learn that their flow can happen in creative contexts—not just in large-scale productions with audience attention but also in their personal self-care. Creating change can happen in many ways, and being creative in finding workarounds can help clear up their overall physical health.

embracing your aura

Hear Your Aura Through Physical Symptoms ·········

When your aura feels stifled and unheard, your body will often do the talking for it. There are many reasons for an ailment, and while seeking medical treatment is the wisest first choice, an accompaniment of energetic healing can help as well. You may have a persistent physical condition that seems to reappear throughout your life. Perhaps it's the series of throat infections the indigo aura may suffer or an uncomfortable bout of constipation the orange aura may dread. Many times, your body will communicate to you what it needs and is lacking through these conditions. The indigo aura feels as if they don't have a voice, while the orange aura is feeling blocked in their goals. In this activity, investigating persistent physical ailments will unlock energetic messages that have been waiting for you to discover them.

TAKING ACTION

1. Reflect upon a persistent illness or ailment you experience. When does this ailment usually occur? What do you do to alleviate it?
2. Consider the symbolic messages this ailment presents to you. How might this issue reflect deeper energetic auric needs and struggles?

Your aura speaks its needs to you all the time, but when it's ignored, it will grab your attention in more physical ways. These conditions can bring major discomfort, the point of which is to force you to understand the discomfort for what it is beyond the physical world.

Visualize Your Aura ·········

The colors around you that make up your energy signature are constantly moving and changing based upon what you are physically going through. It is a living vibration that clings to you, giving the imprint of who you are to all who enter your auric atmosphere. In a visualization, you may notice excess color, rips, or textures that indicate an unhealthy imbalance. Giving yourself a moment to see yourself, really taking the time to contemplate yourself in this way, is intensely validating. The gifts of this visualization practice will be returned by way of a clearer physical well-being. While this practice may not cure the health issues you are experiencing in their entirety, it can give you a sense of identity and a foundation of energy in your physical body.

TAKING ACTION

1. Sit in a quiet spot and take a few deep breaths.
2. When settled, visualize a bright light emanating from all around you.
3. What color is it? What is its shape? How do you consider its overall health?
4. Ask your divine inner wisdom now to show you anything on your physical body that may need healing. Allow that healing to happen as you sit and breathe peacefully.
5. Doing this activity before you go to sleep every night is a helpful self-care routine.

Taking time to acknowledge your aura-body connection with a visualization can be healing and validating for your entire spiritual body. More than anything, it can have special benefits for your physical body, as you are taking the time to validate where it's being affected by any unbalanced energies.

Prioritize Your Health ·········

It may be that you take the time and energy to nurture the health of everyone around you but forget about your own health in the process. The yellow aura might make doctor appointments for their family members but never for themselves. The blue aura might cook according to the dietary needs of a loved one but ignore their own needs or preferences. When you think you are being selfless by taking care of others' needs before your own, you are actually reducing your capacity to continue your caring ways. When you take care of yourself, you are stronger and more able to take care of the people in your life more abundantly than ever. Additionally, you deserve to be a priority on your own list.

TAKING ACTION

1. Consider all the things you do to take care of others in your life.
2. Now ask yourself what you have been putting off doing for yourself.
3. Make yourself the priority! Schedule a medical appointment you've been putting off, cook yourself a healthy meal, or take a brisk walk during your lunch hour.
4. After making yourself the priority, contemplate the ways you feel about the good you have just done. There are no wrong feelings. If you feel guilty, it's time for a closer look at why.

You deserve the same love and attention you give the ones around you. Even when it's not entirely comfortable to make your health a priority, you are sending the same message you do to the ones you are so compassionate and helpful toward: that you are worth the time, energy, and effort it takes to maintain your physical health.

Move Your Body ·········

Your body wants to move, but the ways society tells you to do so may have a detrimental effect. You may overhear your friends talking about the latest workout craze, be tempted to purchase an expensive piece of equipment for your home, or see the way social media influencers are getting their bodies in shape. All of these inputs can cause you to feel overwhelmed, stopping you before you take your first aerobic step forward! Luckily, your aura has ways in which it is more motivated to move than others. You may notice that as a red aura, lifting weights is empowering, or as a blue aura, walks with a friend seem to work out better than anything else. Your green aura may crave getting lost in nature, or your yellow aura may enjoy the local salsa class. No matter what way you feel most comfortable moving, leaning into your aura and knowing that the purpose of movement is to feed your body will help you create a lasting habit.

TAKING ACTION

1. Get creative by trying out a variety of physical exercises!
2. Afterward, ask yourself what feelings accompanied your favorite physical activities. Think about these feelings before, during, and afterward.
3. Reflect on how the activities you find both pleasurable and good for your physical health relate to your aura.
4. Think about ways to incorporate these exercises into your day-to-day life in a way that does not feel overwhelming to you. Stick these activities on your calendar or schedule them with a friend who will give you lots of encouragement to keep it up.

Understanding your aura can help you choose some physical fitness activities that are more authentic to you.

Use Healthy Mantras ·········

Our auras tend to be affected by the ways we speak in our minds and the perceptions we have of life. When we speak to ourselves harshly, our auras can signal their need for love and attention through our physical bodies. The yellow aura who harshly critiques themselves for not being perfect may become saddled with intense neck pain. The purple aura who struggles with procrastination may be riddled with extreme bouts of anxiety. Listening to the way you speak to yourself is the first step toward understanding how to not only address the issue but also soften or support it where needed. Using mantras is an effective way to mindfully replace those repetitive thoughts that may not be serving you with ones that actually do.

TAKING ACTION

1. For the next whole day, pay attention to your self-talk. Reflect on the common patterns and themes that emerge.
2. In what ways do these patterns relate to your physical needs?
3. Create a positive mantra that can be used to replace the self-talk that no longer serves you. Saying "I am strong" while struggling to get active, or "My body is a gift to me" when looking in the mirror are easy mantras to use until you create one that works for you long term.
4. Write this mantra where you can see it often, and repeat it to yourself out loud several times each day until you feel it has become a happy habit.

The words we say to ourselves matter, for they help create the stability of the physical body in which we live. Our bodies are directly affected by our attitudes toward ourselves and are far better able to rise to the challenges we give them when we speak more kindly to ourselves.

Make Playtime a Priority ·········

Being healthy isn't just about eating right and working out; it's also about finding ways to be truly present and joyful in the everyday moments. The ability to connect to joy promotes health and wellness. As a child, you were able to find joy often and in natural ways. Perhaps you were the pink aura child who created magical worlds in which you played for hours on end. It could be that you were the indigo child who got lost in books, feeling able to carry yourself to the lands you read about. Connecting to that childlike joy is how you can bring it into your life now.

TAKING ACTION

1. Think about yourself as a child: What brought you pure and simple joy?
2. Reflect on a time in your life when you last felt a similar feeling. How long ago was this? If you can't remember, how does that make you feel?
3. What is a simple way you can feel a moment of joy? Do this activity today.
4. Take a moment to connect this moment of joy with your aura colors. What does this experience reveal about you?
5. Brainstorm ways you can create more of these moments in your daily life. Make calendar reminders for yourself or enlist a supportive friend to make sure you stick to it.

A joyful act of physical care goes hand in hand with connecting to your aura. On the journey to recapturing your joy and prioritizing your health, you'll find another treasure: yourself.

Practice Meditation ·········

Many studies show that meditation has numerous positive effects on health, like decreasing blood pressure, improving heart rate, and having a positive long-term effect on brain function. Meditation can look like many things for different auras. A yellow aura with a busy mind may benefit from guided meditation, whereas a red aura may prefer listening to soft instrumental music to promote calm. Following your preferences is essential to finding a meditation practice you will stick with.

TAKING ACTION

1. With the knowledge you have about your aura, reflect on meditation techniques and tools that may be helpful to you. Also consider what hasn't worked in past meditation experiences and how you might avoid these obstacles.

2. Give yourself a short-term goal of a consistent meditation practice. Three to five days to set a consistent schedule is a perfectly acceptable start.

3. Set a timer for five minutes (over time, you can lengthen your meditations as you prefer). Lie or sit in a comfortable position. Close your eyes if possible.

4. Breathe steadily and start repeating a mantra that resonates with you. "I am peace" is a helpful starting mantra.

5. When you feel ready, open your eyes and come out of the meditation.

6. After each of these meditations, reflect on how you physically feel since embarking on this new meditation journey.

You are a connected being, and giving yourself the time to explore that connection is a way to improve wellness.

Perform a Physical Healing ·········

Energy is always moving through your body, and you have more power than you know when it comes to regulating its flow. Taking control over your energetic body will directly and positively affect your physical one, and with practice, you can become quite adept at it. The green aura may find that a mindful walking meditation connects them to their life-force energy, while a turquoise aura may prefer a foot bath with special crystals. The point is to create a mindful experience that validates your mind-body connection in a way that simply feels good.

TAKING ACTION

1. Consider an actionable way you find calmness. Think about what you want to do to feel relaxed, calm, and centered.
2. Brainstorm ways to level up this experience so you can speak to your authentic energy. Use mystical tools, reflection practices, or creative outlets that engage your aura colors.
3. Find a quiet time to perform your physical healing now, analyzing how you feel before, during, and after the practice.

You have more power to heal than you may realize. Giving yourself the gift of self-healing simply by allocating the space, time, and actions that honor it is greatly rewarding and medicinal.

CHAPTER 7

· · · · · · · · · · · ·

Auras and Relationships

Energy is an exchange, and relationships are the ultimate context in which this exchange is demonstrated in our lives. The pieces of ourselves in which we send our love to a friend or significant other are delivered through our aura. The ways we present ourselves, show others we care, and receive information from the people we hold affection for can be better understood and refined when we have auric insight attached to them. Reviewing your relationships through the lens of the aura colors of loved ones also provides a more detailed understanding of them and how *they* energetically operate. It can be easier to let something go or make something work with the energetic wisdom your knowledge of auras provides. And when it comes to compatibility, your aura colors are the key to understanding what is hit or miss for you within romantic dynamics. In this chapter, you will be able to reflect upon the myriad relationships in your life, romantic, friendship, and familial, and begin creating more honest and fulfilling connections.

What Your Aura Says about You

Each aura values relationships and approaches relationship situations in a unique way.

· · · · · **RED** · · · · ·

In the context of relationships, red auras look to themselves to provide and protect. And in their never-ending quest to create places for others to thrive and feel safe, they often consider themselves to be leaders and decision-makers. The red aura's takeover attitude is their way of showing love, as actions mean more to them than meaningless verbal sentiments. Red auras in romantic contexts are passionate and ask for respect and loyalty. In dating, they prefer an action setting, such as ice-skating or a friendly competition of darts. They like to take people out of their comfort zone to see how they react and feel a raw connection in these situations. In friendship connections, they enjoy forming a cohesive and tight friend group. They don't usually have separate friend groups but rather will merge them together. In friendships and love connections alike, they back up their feelings with outward expressions and are usually the ones offering to pay for a meal or take over the running of a household's financial matters. While they do not shy away from expressing their emotions, the feelings they have can run hot and intense. It's very difficult for a red aura to be anything less than honest, so in their relationships, they often say what they mean quickly and directly, giving transparent feedback and answering questions in a way that could be considered abrupt or forward. The red aura doesn't want to leave space for any interpretation; they prefer to control the perception of every relationship, as they prefer to control all things in life. Red auras have a loyal mindset; once they set their heart upon someone, they don't ever let it stray.

····· **BLUE** ·····

Blue auras are consistently assessing others' emotions and wants for ways to assist and lend compassion. Blue auras are made for relationships, as they understand the meaning of the word "compromise" and have been living their life this way for as long as they can remember. They don't mind giving in to others or living with a little less due to the other person's needs in a relationship. In fact, they prefer it this way. Yet over time without introspection, they can find themselves feeling resentful, invisible, and exhausted. Blue auras are often so giving that they put a wall up against anyone who might reciprocate—leaving the people they love without any sort of insight on how to even do so. It's difficult to buy a blue aura person a gift or find a way to show any gesture of gratitude, as they are uncomfortable being the receivers. In romantic relationships, a little bit goes a long way with a blue aura. They love a sweet gesture that isn't over the top, and they find it genuine when someone takes the time to simply share emotions. A quiet evening together is the ideal date for a blue aura, as they love spending quality time with the people they love in comfort. In friendships, blue auras love to show support and work as a team to get things done. Helping a friend meet their steps goal on a weekend walk or getting together for a social potluck allows the blue aura to feel connected.

····· YELLOW ·····

Life doesn't come with a guidebook, but it does come with yellow auras. The yellow aura in any relationship naturally creates the pathways of least resistance out of any challenge thrown their way. In romantic relationships, yellow auras can move faster than most in planning ahead when they meet someone they connect to. They seek consistency and organization and will bring others into this way of thinking to show their devotion. The ideal date is one that reflects thought and planning. A surprise dinner at a restaurant where they specifically mentioned they've never been shows the yellow aura that they've been heard and considered. In friendships, yellow auras love being the one who plans the dream trip everyone wants to go on. Yellow auras don't shy away from a crisis or a tough time; they provide empathy and understanding through helpful actions and decisive moves. Often, yellow auras can be perceived in relationships as being cold or unfeeling because their first reaction in any partnership is to do the most logical thing: take in information and get busy providing solutions. They aren't always ones to show emotion, but they will quietly and carefully take on what anyone needs them to without a complaint. Yellow auras are stable people in an unstable world, yet they can be cast aside quickly once a problem is fixed—only to be called in again when needed. This can lead to them feeling their efforts are unappreciated. Learning how to vulnerably communicate their needs in a relationship is the journey the yellow aura often takes, however odd it feels at first for them to do so.

· · · · · PURPLE · · · · ·

Purple auras want to grow, and they crave dynamic environments in which to force themselves into change. Relationships are one way purple auras seek evolution. Purple auras like a variety of energies and perspectives; they enjoy interesting people from all walks of life. Purple auras don't fear dark truths or vulnerabilities, but they do fear stagnancy. A relationship for a purple aura must be one in which there is movement, and because of this, long-term relationships that fall into a rut can take their toll on the purple aura's emotional state. Any lasting relationship for them includes a flow of ideas and feedback and a joint willingness to embark on new adventures. In romantic relationships, there is much focus on passion and fireworks, which sometimes can confuse the purple auras as to the purpose of this connection. They tend to fall hard and fast for love interests and very seldom hesitate in stating their intentions. The ideal date for a purple aura is one where there is room for spontaneity. A lawn concert with a festival to follow feeds the purple aura's need to experience excitement with a partner and showcases their own adaptability in any environment. In friendships, they enjoy last-minute weekends away with little to no game plan, allowing for the mood of the moment to direct what activities will follow. Purple auras don't fear being hurt, as they see both pain and joy as necessary components to living a full and vibrant life. Purple auras are fun, and they entertain anyone lucky enough to have them in their lives, but they also have to understand that the truths they seek are already within them.

····· GREEN ·····

There is a calming vibration that many of us crave, and green auras bring that to any relationship. Green auras are able to separate the emotions that can distract from reality and cause discord, and because of that, they are wonderful companions to those who have a hard time doing the same. Green auras are uniquely able to see the world as a series of interconnected systems, and in a relationship, they strive for comprehension and ways to improve the flow of its design. Because green auras are uniquely able to self-contain their thoughts and emotions, they must be reminded that not everyone has this ability. The perfect date for a green aura involves a thoughtful combination of intellect and adventure. A wine-tasting paired with fusion cuisine allows for both entertainment and intelligent conversation. When spending time with friends, the green aura loves to be in a context of like-minded individuals, often exchanging ideas and getting excited about the nuances of whatever specific interest, recent research, or field of study they all have in common. The journey for the green aura in any friendship or romantic relationship is to check in on the ways the other person thinks and feels rather than seeing everything from their own perspective alone. Early in romantic relationships, green auras are intense and emotive, making sure their feelings are known and the vision they see for their future partnership is clear. Over time, their words can taper off, leaving their partners to wonder if they still feel the same.

Expressing feelings is always a necessary practice and is one green auras should pay particular attention to. Green auras are peaceful energies; they crave a sense of stability in this ever-changing world. Giving the people they love this same sense of system and foundation is their way of showing love.

····· INDIGO ·····

For indigo auras, relationships are micro universes. The feelings and emotions surrounding them have a cosmic impact on the indigo aura's self-worth, feelings, and outlook on life. Indigo auras are naturally highly perceptive of not only others' thoughts and emotions but also the root causes of these thoughts and emotions. Thus, indigo auras are constantly attempting to softly uncover wounds and unsaid feelings to heal the ones they love. Romance for indigo auras is a peaceful connection. They enjoy feeling safe and at home with their partner. In these love connections, they require balance and don't always need verbal reassurances of the bond they share. An ideal date for the indigo aura is one where their romantic interest is acquainting them with one of their interests, such as sightseeing in a part of town they grew up in or introducing them to their favorite pastime. Because of the indigo aura's intense ability to connect, they likely have strong yet few friendships. Since they expend so much emotional and spiritual energy on the people they bring into their innermost circle, they cannot have many people in this circle at one time, favoring smaller groups or one-on-one interactions. They prefer an in-depth conversation with a friend over a cup of tea to a wild night on the town. When over-whelmed, they may disappear from friendships to repair their energetic boundaries. Indigos are quiet creatures, energetically cloaking themselves against the louder and more vibrant forces in their surroundings. But to know an indigo is to understand the depth at which they flow and how being with them pulls anyone else into an undertow of deep reflection and cocoon-like safety.

· · · · · PINK · · · · ·

The pink aura exists in a world of their own creation. While they don't enjoy leaving this place, they are more than happy to let others in who share the enthusiasm and joy that they do. Pink auras are optimistic energies, bringing with them their own view of life that they wish for their relationships to have as well. In close connections, they epitomize rose-colored glasses, silver linings, and the bright side of everything. Those who can truly appreciate this are often overtaken by the pink aura's charming vibration and magical interpretation of the world. Romantic connections for a pink aura are about unity and peace. They enjoy talking about how to make every moment count and need a partner who finds this discourse invigorating and not immature. A pink aura dream date consists of a thematic, thoughtful endeavor, such as a drive-in movie followed by milkshakes and burgers at the local soda bar or a quaint picnic in a picturesque area. Friendships with a pink aura are often full of surprises, as they love to bring their companions along on their planned escapes from reality. Taking their friends to brunch followed by a spa day or a night out to a VIP lounge are some of the ways pink auras show their friends love and attention. Pink auras are often ridiculed for their bubbly energy, and in relationships, they must be watchful for anyone who tries to capture their unique magic and take it away as their own. Many times, pink auras can feel isolated and misunderstood, not understanding how they came to be at the place in a relationship where they trigger others. The pink aura's journey is about loving who they are in a mindful and self-aware way so that they can choose others who equally appreciate this ability.

· · · · · TURQUOISE · · · · ·

Turquoise auras are mirror holders in relationships: They show the other person who they are in an attempt to give them essential and life-altering insights. Because of this, the people they partner with might project their own self-loathing upon the turquoise auras, causing them pain and confusion. Without understanding their reflective ability, the turquoise aura can feel confused about who they are, and the relationship can suffer for it. But with mindful understanding of this gift, turquoise auras can verbalize their contributions to their loved one's healing and better explain their reasons behind it. Turquoise auras are loving, giving, and helping people. In romantic relationships, they want a lifestyle that reflects their own openness and adaptability. A perfect date for a turquoise aura is one where they can be in an adaptable and invigorating environment. A music festival with seats on the lawn or a day of green market shopping with local vendors are both fun first-time connections for the turquoise aura to not only be themselves but also to see their partner as they are. Outings with friends should be movement-based as well, as the turquoise aura seems to balance best with others when in motion. Garage sale hopping or a day of volunteering provides turquoise auras with the context they feel most themselves in. Honest and open conversations, emotional exchanges, and prioritizing energetic connections over material possessions are ways turquoise auras feel solid in a partnership. The turquoise aura's journey in any relationship is to immerse themselves in a sea of energetic connection and be able to pick out the threads of who they are versus what they are trying to show the other person.

····· ORANGE ·····

Orange auras find romance and friendships to be imperative. Solid foundations, structures of support, and loyal connections are all part of the orange aura's vision of what a complete life entails. Orange auras view relationships as multitasking entities; therefore, they often mix work and love together. Creating businesses with friends, placing people who are loyal to them in strategic places, and creating bonds that surpass the constraints of any other code interests them. Orange auras have no problem using relationships to get ahead, and they see this as a normal and preferred way to get to where they want to go. They are very honest about it and make it clear to the people entering this arrangement what is expected of them. Romantic relationships for the orange aura are about a shared dream, one in which the orange aura's partner is just as enthusiastic about similar goals. They tend to be very romantic and are big on gestures that display their larger-than-life affection. An ideal date for an orange aura consists of showing exactly how much they enjoy their date's company by way of a fancy dinner or coveted sideline tickets to the big game. In friendships, they aren't subtle about how they show their gratitude. They will arrange large group outings complete with transportation and top-notch service. Getting their friends private access to clubs and events is something orange auras will pull strings to do. When an orange aura wins at life, the people in their relationships seem to feel the same sense of success, as they feel tied to the person they helped journey there.

embracing
your aura

Do a First Date Self-Analysis · · · · · · · ·

Whether it's been a while or is something you do often, first dates can be very energetically enlightening. The energy you project to a person you wish to connect with while on a first date can be intended one way by you and interpreted completely differently by the other party. If you are a yellow aura, you might intend to be curious but come off more intrusive. Or you could feel so uncomfortable talking about yourself that you exude a mysterious and shy vibration, as a blue aura can sometimes do. Thinking about the energetic first impression you give in a romantic setting is a strong lens through which to see your auric energy at work—and a first step toward adapting behavior for more successful dates in the future.

TAKING ACTION

1. Think about a time you were on a first date. What were your fears? What were you excited about? How do you feel you acted out your own energy to the other person? Do you think their perspective of you aligned with what you intended to show them?
2. Reflect on the ways in which your first date behavior and intentions connect to your aura and how you can see things differently if you look at them from another perspective.

Understanding how you see yourself versus how others may perceive you is helpful insight in your journey to becoming your most authentic self, both in and out of relationships.

Start a Club ·········

It's easy to lose track of where people are when everyone is so busy. Deeper conversations can take more time and aren't always feasible to keep up. Just because you can't communicate with all the people you love doesn't mean you don't want to. Creating an online meetup with a goal, such as a book, movie, or fitness club, is one way you can keep in contact without the upkeep of individual conversations. Letting your friends take turns choosing the goals for your scheduled meetups will be very aurically revealing! You may find the indigo auras choosing the insightful reads for a book discussion and the yellow auras suggesting a recipe exchange. Having fun conversations about these topics gives everyone the connections they crave and the energetic insight into one another.

TAKING ACTION

1. Choose a club and determine this month's goal and meetup times.
2. Create a schedule for who is in charge of each month's meeting and allow ample time for discussions and planning.
3. Have fun! How do you feel connected to your friends through this activity?
4. What do you notice about their aura colors and their points of view? See if they can discuss it among themselves!

You've loved many people throughout your life from different seasons and times. Your relationships past, present, and future can feel scattered and hard to keep up with. Having a meetup for everyone and allowing their authentic energetic selves to take the lead with some group goals is a great way to continue to get to know them.

Revisit Past Relationships ·········

Some relationships come into our lives and don't work out for one reason or another. Thinking about the exes in your life and reflecting upon their imperfections and incompatibilities is a normal part of breakup reflection. Another way to look at it is not focusing on what was wrong with them or the relationship but considering what your needs were at the time you chose them. A blue aura who is too shy to speak up may choose a partner who never seems to stop talking. A red aura who is used to taking charge may constantly be dating partners who don't seem to be able to get their lives together. Mindfully following the past romantic connections in your life can lead you to priceless insight for future connections.

TAKING ACTION

1. Reflect thoughtfully on the exes in your life. What are the common stand-out issues that made the relationships crumble?
2. Thinking of one of these issues, ask yourself what part of you initially ignored or was okay with it, and why. Allow yourself to get vulnerable with these insights and identify what aura traits may have been at play.
3. Praise yourself for this vulnerable reflection.

The parts of your aura that need to be honored, respected, and validated can be found in the times in relationships when they weren't. There can be a danger of choosing people who seemingly fill a void that in fact needs to be self-fulfilled.

Appreciate Your Lasting Friendships ·········

Friends are some of life's greatest blessings. In a very large and sometimes lonely world, friendships can make us feel safe and accepted. They are based on choice, which allows for a sense of energetic freedom. The friend who applauds your purple aura ability to be the first one to sing at karaoke or the friend who knows just what to buy you even though your blue aura self never feels comfortable asking for things are the ones who see *you*— the real you. Expressing your ability to see a friend the way they see you helps show them another layer of your appreciation and love.

TAKING ACTION

1. Consider a friend in your life who has been a stable figure for you.
2. What do you feel when you are around them? How do they show you that they care? How do those actions show you that they understand the true you?
3. Now think about this friend in terms of their energetic imprint: What do you feel their aura colors are? You could even have them take the quiz in Part 1 (without telling them what it's for)!
4. Based on their aura colors, determine a way to show them that you see them the way they aurically are. Take them on an outing, give them a gift, or have a meaningful conversation centered around how you see their authentic self.

Demonstrating to your friends that you can see their true energetic selves is a gift that permeates the soul and makes your connections even stronger.

Date for Your Aura ·········

Whether you are in a relationship or on the lookout for one, it's time to put what you know about your aura to good use. Allowing your aura to lead the way on your next dating adventure is a great way to explore your strengths—and dabble outside your comfort zone to find new ones. Perhaps allowing your green aura to plan a romantic hiking adventure in a local park will give you and your date that next-level connection. Or letting your turquoise aura invite a romantic interest on your next indie bookstore shopping adventure will allow this special person to catch glimpses of the authentic you. With your aura colors in mind, allow yourself to think of activities where you can shine.

TAKING ACTION

1. Brainstorm some activities for dates in an environment you feel most comfortable in and invite someone to come along with you.
2. Awkwardness is normal—be sure to let your date know that this is new for you too!
3. The success of the date is determined by how you felt during it. Afterward, reflect thoughtfully and kindly on your highs and lows during the date and how doing this made you feel more authentically you.

Getting more vulnerable with yourself by taking the initiative on a date is not only about being true to yourself; you're also permitting another person to see the real you.

Let Go of Control ·········

Control in relationships can play out in different ways; for example, how the household is run, what holiday traditions happen, or where you are having dinner. However it is looked at, control is about keeping things in a space where we feel the most comfortable. The way you exhibit control in relationships can vary depending on your aura color. The indigo aura may want to limit the number of people coming to a holiday party because they won't feel up to the task of making sure everyone is comfortable. Or the orange aura may find it impossible to be on a family vacation without signing off on the exact itinerary. Control can be quiet or loud, but understanding where you hold it in a relationship can help you let it go when necessary for the health of your connections.

TAKING ACTION

1. Think back upon a time you didn't have control. What did that feel like?
2. When considering all the feelings that came up in this situation, reflect on how your answers connect to your aura colors.
3. Practice letting go of control over one small thing in your life today.
4. Reflect upon how it feels to let go of control.
5. Continue practicing letting go, working up to larger things as you get more skilled.

Using the situations in which you feel uncomfortable and out of control to further your introspective journey allows you to create more control in the most important place there is: your auric field.

Rekindle Your Romance ·········

Long-term romantic connections need regular attention to keep the energy of the partnership alive and fresh. Life is busy, and a disconnect in the relationship can begin to form. Instead of sharing energy, creating space for each other to grow, and finding new ways to inspire each other, you can begin to go through the motions and take each other for granted. Thinking about how to rekindle your romance through the lens of aura colors is a fun way to get the connection back up and running. The yellow aura could plan a fun date night of golf for their green aura partner, or a blue aura could cook a favorite treat their red aura partner especially loves. Whatever the rekindling involves, doing it in a way that both communicates love to your partner's unique energy signature and represents your own is how that love is refreshed.

TAKING ACTION

1. Reflect upon what your partner's aura colors are.
2. Think of something you can do to show them you care in a way you know they will be able to receive it.
3. Rekindle that romance! As you do so, be mindful of how it feels when you show a person that you really see and love them for who they are.

In a life where we are often praised for the things we do for others, it's nice to be seen for the person we are within—the motivating factor behind it all. Showing your partner you see them is always a romantic gesture.

Check Your Aura Compatibility •••••••••

You aren't always going to be compatible with everyone. When you understand that this has a lot to do with your energetic signature, it can save you time and trouble when dating. Being real with yourself as to who works for you and who doesn't, and why, gives you clarity into what choices to make on the dating scene. As an orange aura, you may realize you need more of a supporting partner than a person wanting to make it on their own. A turquoise aura may feel the need to be with someone who places little to no emphasis on the material world and enjoys spiritual pursuits.

TAKING ACTION

1. On a blank piece of paper, make a chart where you can fill in your insights from the following steps. Create at least three rows, with room to add more rows and/or notes later.
2. Reflect upon what you like and dislike in people; don't fear being honest with yourself.
3. Consider what your strengths contribute to a relationship and how your more vulnerable qualities need to be supported.
4. Looking at what you've written, contemplate what type of person would fit you best. Be specific about their goals, character traits, and ways of acting.
5. Visualize what the perfect partner would be. Keep this visualization to how you feel with them, not how they look.

Getting a better idea of what energies you work best with helps attract them to you. A clear and focused intention allows for the people who fit you, and you them, to instantly attract.

CHAPTER 8

. . . .

Auras and Money and Career

You were born to express yourself in your most authentic way possible, and one way to do that is through your career. When you understand your aura, and your unique energetic motivations, strengths, and ways of doing things that make sense to you, you can choose a career that enriches your very soul. Work becomes a beautiful expression of your individual energy. You feel assured in life. Money is energy too—an energy that represents gratitude, value, self-worth, and above all a way to continue living a life that serves you and others. When you view money as a result of how well you are living your most authentic energy, its accumulation isn't as hard to conceive. The more you do what you came here to do based on your unique auric imprint—the more you lean into your unique energy— the more you will be attracting energy in the form of professional and financial abundance. In this chapter, you will uncover those connections between what you do regarding work and finances and who you truly are.

What Your Aura Says about You

Each aura values money in a unique way and has a different view of what a successful career looks like for them.

····· RED ·····

Red auras enjoy being in control in a career and welcome the challenges and responsibilities that accompany that position. Red auras often prefer strong leadership positions in which they can facilitate team-building, healthy competition, and growth. They feel very strongly about respect, both receiving it and giving it. Red auras are very fair and don't shirk the uncomfortable parts of managing others, such as redirecting or giving constructive criticism. They make the more difficult decisions with their own moral compass and system of logic and expect them to be tested. They are often drawn to positions such as firefighters, police officers, and servicepeople. For red auras, money is about function; they welcome it to further their ability to grow the teams and brands they put their heart into. Receiving abundance feels better when it is hard won, and red auras must be careful not to dismiss more easily earned abundance. For a red aura, legacy is important. They want something to embody the hard work they've put in and carry it on past their own lives. Therefore, they are as protective of the positions they hold as they are of the people in their lives they feel responsible for. A red aura knows that they are going to have to make the tough choices, and they prefer that to being at the whim of others.

····· BLUE ·····

Blue auras are drawn to help and heal others in this lifetime, and a career is often looked at as a way to further this goal rather than to earn credit or money. Because blue auras are often seen as such selfless givers who take their compensation from the joy they can manifest in others, they can be ignored by the professional world regarding payment, value, and promotion. Blue auras are often drawn to teaching, nursing, and therapy but can also find fulfillment managing a busy office or stepping in to make a space run smoothly and easing the burdens of others. Because they are so concerned with creating joy and peace among those they assist, they can feel shame at receiving abundance in the form of money, as they can associate taking it with taking away from their ultimate motivating factor of helping others. Blue auras need to learn that money can create a context in which their helpful work can not only continue but also be easier to facilitate in their own lives. Blue auras can feel burned out and overlooked in their jobs, and because of that, they can feel as if they are to be blamed. Learning how to receive gratitude is the necessary journey a blue aura must take.

· · · · · YELLOW · · · · ·

In a world of chaos and disorder, the yellow aura feels compelled to step in and create flow. Yellow auras enjoy using their natural skills of organization in their careers. They prefer working alone. In jobs where leadership and teamwork are required, they tend to lean on the tools they create, such as flowcharts or schedules, to outsource their ideas and make everyone self-sufficient. They often work in management as directors or as solo entrepreneurs tasked with complicated projects that require a lot of focus. Yellow auras have a creative eye; combined with their ability to form ideas, they can be interior designers, real estate agents, and event planners. Yellow auras have no problem receiving money; however, they often find multiple ways to send it out in the world as soon as they obtain it. Because they are astutely able to foresee the connections to be made in their networks, they see all the ways their money can be spent to reach new levels of interest. Patience not being a huge virtue, they consider money to be a means to an end and not something to sit on or wait for.

· · · · · PURPLE · · · · ·

Purple auras understand that work is for living, but it's not life. Because of their need for change, they often have a difficult time committing to one career path for their entire lives. Needing a dynamic atmosphere to feel their most comfortable, change is a source of inner stability. Purple auras must be wary of how society views their multiple career changes. This is authentic to the way they work, but it can appear flaky to others. Purple auras look to the environment where they are working rather than the job requirements, prioritizing flexibility of schedule, the vibe of the workplace, and whether they will be micromanaged. They enjoy feeling the freedom to create while challenging themselves to thrive in chaotic environments. Because of this, they often go into artistic industries, fashion, and food service. For a purple aura, money is about freedom; they take as much as they need to get to the next level and feel unrestricted. They tend to worry less about money than they do their own constraints and therefore can be forgetful and unmindful of it as a downfall. Purple auras often see money as something they are enslaved to, and in their abundantly rebellious vibration, they will reject it as such.

· · · · · GREEN · · · · ·

The world around us has numerous interconnected systems, many of which we are a part of but are not always able to see. Green auras specialize in venturing behind the curtain into the inner workings of all that creates society and the universe we call home. Green auras choose careers that challenge their brilliant minds. They seek out complicated questions and throw themselves with unrivaled focus into the quest for answers. Therefore, green auras often have careers in engineering, science, and research. They have an eagle's-eye view of the bigger picture and can place themselves in positions to act as puppeteers in the universe. Producing and innovating are their fortes, as they enjoy reinventing and reworking what has already been done but that can be improved. Oftentimes, they find themselves as connectors, bridge makers of sorts, for channels of communication between one system and another. For a green aura, money is simply about the ability to continue their work. Because they enjoy their focus, money tends to follow them in maintaining it. Green auras care little about material items; instead, they can both receive and repel money based on where they are mentally. The green aura's relationship with money must be connected to the enterprises they love so they can prioritize their preferred tasks.

· · · · · INDIGO · · · · ·

Indigo auras are solitary creatures who love to help and coordinate the healing of others, often to a point of total life change. To do this, they require an intense connection to the people and contexts they assist. The indigo aura's ability to see into the parts of individuals and systems that are broken and in need of repair is unrivaled, but it also requires intense focus and energy output. Therefore, indigos must work independently or one-on-one to align their energies with their life purpose in a career. They are drawn to specialized healing practices such as speech-language pathology, hospice care, and child therapy. Because they require so much attention for such a specialized focus, they can often feel like they aren't doing as much as their peers in terms of output. However, for an indigo, it's the quality of work and not the quantity that should be measured. Receiving money can feel uncomfortable to an indigo aura, as they often don't feel deserving of it because of the limiting belief they have about their skills. Indigo auras must understand that the work they do, even if it's just for one person or place, is oftentimes life changing and worthy of abundance and gratitude.

····· PINK ·····

Pink auras choose their career based on the same principles they use to choose everything in life: by prioritizing their joy. They are often underestimated because of their perceived naiveté and superficiality, but they actually have an incredible eye for detail and design. Pink auras are naturally creative and have no problem finding the pieces in our world that are overlooked but that hold untapped potential. Therefore, they are often trendsetters who create new ways to grab attention. Because of this, seeing them in marketing positions, influencer jobs, and the fashion world is not uncommon. Since their style is often unorthodox, they can be dismissed by many as they approach a task or creative project. Being allowed to work on their own and self-advocate for their independence in this way is crucial to their success. A pink aura sees money as something to be manifested when needed. They tend to have no fear of wanting the things they find beautiful and necessary, and much like children, they can wish it into their reality. They receive gifts without hesitation and spend without too much thought of consequences. Pink auras can compartmentalize reality in their focus on joy, making budgeting a real challenge. Pink auras have the task in this lifetime of connecting how they find their joy to how they create a living for themselves. When the two align, pink auras are an inspiration to many who wish to do the same.

····· TURQUOISE ·····

Not many people can tap into the interconnectedness of all people. However, turquoise auras reign freely in the space between us all, waiting to find ways to support others. Turquoise auras are often called to heal in new and unique ways. They have a natural ability to shine a light on pathways to healing, love, and a sense of purpose. Thus, turquoise auras tend to flock to holistic curative professions such as acupuncturists, energy healers, and doulas. They must advocate for themselves in any workspace, and therefore, choosing careers in which they are labeled as the expert will build their confidence. Turquoise auras' attitude toward money is a collective one, as they have a "take what you need and leave the rest" approach. But this attitude can leave them always needing or wanting a little more than they've been given, and their self-worth can suffer as a result. Turquoise auras are so used to being absorbed in the work the people they connect with do that they forget their own important role in facilitating it. They must remind themselves that they, too, are allowed to tap into the healing they so generously provide to others and receive compensation for the contexts they create in which healing happens.

· · · · · ORANGE · · · · ·

There is power in the world that few feel the need to aspire to; orange auras have no fear or limitation when it comes to reaching for this power. Orange auras are fascinated by the sense of energy that comes with unlimited resources, a sense of command, and endless abundance. They crave finding ways to express themselves in arenas of power and will stop at nothing to achieve influence. Their fearlessness can be seen as recklessness by others, and they are often underestimated at the start of their careers. Luckily, the orange aura is able to shut out naysaying voices that undermine their goals. Sometimes, these voices even fuel their determination. Orange auras like being in command and don't much care for the opinions of the ones they lead. They often are drawn to positions such as venture capitalists, entrepreneurs, and political leaders. For the orange aura, money plays the part of image and assistant. They use it and spend it freely to keep themselves moving higher up the ladder. Money will be used to break through any obstacle they encounter and also to forge contacts and favors. Orange auras are relentless in their pursuit of things that inspire awe in others. They aim to always be the one on top.

embracing your aura

Do a Past Jobs Reflection ·········

The jobs you've had in the past may have felt varied, but they likely had some elements in common. In each of them, you showcased your unique auric energy. As a blue aura, perhaps you didn't mind dealing with difficult customers at a retail job. As a purple aura, you might have enjoyed dressing up the mannequins at the dress shop you worked in. You may have been valued because of your talent with balancing books as a yellow aura or praised for your ability to finally fix the Wi-Fi connection at the office as a green aura. The things you were talented at in past positions provide valuable insight for creating your career goals now.

TAKING ACTION

1. Reflect upon all the past jobs you've had. Choose a few that stand out to you.
2. Identify the more fun elements (or, at least, the more tolerable) of these jobs.
3. Consider the overall trend in past jobs regarding what you were good at and preferred doing.
4. Connect these talents to your aura.
5. Write down some jobs that would list these talents as requirements or preferred skills. Use the Internet to help you brainstorm, if needed.

The parts of a job in which you found satisfaction and joy can create a better focus for future careers that suit you, aligning with your aura and supporting your life purpose.

Want Something ·········

It can be a very scary thing to want something. This is because disappointment in not receiving it is something you might fear and have been taught to avoid. But it's okay to want. In fact, you should. Wanting things that fulfill you and allow you to express your auric self is what you deserve and what you are supposed to have. As an orange aura, you may be looking to the corner office at your current company. As a green aura, maybe the funding for that research you've been dreaming of is calling your name. For this activity, all you need to do is unlock your desire and freethinking to manifest the things you want.

TAKING ACTION

1. Take a moment and enter a relaxed and focused state away from any distractions.
2. Think about what you really want in life.
3. With your eyes open or closed, visualize how your day would look if you had what you wanted—the routine and abundance that surrounds you in this reality.
4. Now ask yourself: "What does it feel like to have everything I want? How do the people in my life benefit from me being this fulfilled? How does it feel to express myself as authentically as I can in this situation?"
5. Take this feeling and carry it with you moving forward. Know that you did a brave thing: You put something you want out there in the universe. Think about how you can align every choice to your authentic aura self as you did in your visualization.

Through this visualization, you are linking your ability to make money to your self-worth and inviting abundance to come to you.

Consider Your Current Job ·········

Your current job, or the job you most recently had, can provide insight into your aura. You most likely thrive in contexts that enhance your authentic energy, and you may feel depleted in environments that require you to be something you're not. Green auras may feel vibrant and excited about what they are learning today in their career but will be bored if it's too monotonous. Blue auras feel drained if they are asked to give others constructive criticism, but they are joyful when they get to see how their work helps someone directly.

TAKING ACTION

1. Think about the parts of your job you find the most draining. Be specific when you think about this.
2. Reflect on specific tasks, incidents, and responsibilities that created negative feelings. What was going on? Why did you feel this way? How did it misalign with who you are intrinsically?
3. Compare these tasks to your aura colors and identify the reasons why this work was more challenging for you energetically.
4. Consider where you can take some energy away (even if it's only a little) from these more draining aspects of your job. Is there another way you can complete a task, or is there a more appropriate person it could be delegated to?

Homing in on which parts of your present job are the most favorable and which parts are the most unfavorable is going to highlight your inner workings. You may find yourself reflecting on putting energy toward finding a new job that suits you better. When you choose a job that makes you feel energized instead of mentally exhausted, you connect more closely to your purpose and become the best version of yourself.

Explore Your Money Mindset ·········

The relationship you have with money is unique to you. The way you were raised, the programming you received from society, and any financial traumas you endured can be seen in the way you think about, use, and receive money. Taking control over your money mindset happens once you understand your aura colors. If you are a blue aura, you might feel ashamed about collecting money for your service job. As a red aura, you could have a hard time accepting money if you feel it wasn't earned. Leaning into your aura will help you be more intentional in your relationship with and beliefs about money

TAKING ACTION

1. Think about a time you received money for doing a job you actually liked to do. How did it feel to receive that money? How did you use it?
2. Reflect on a time you received money for a job you didn't care for. How did it feel receiving that money? How did you use it?
3. Consider how you felt about these two instances and what it says about your relationship with money.
4. Mindfully think about what these two instances may be linked to in your past programming or traumas you have endured.
5. Ask yourself, "What is my value to others? How does the answer relate to my aura colors?"

Society wants to tell you which jobs are worth receiving money for and which are not, as well as how to use that money, but it's up to you to make those decisions. When you connect to money as an energetic exchange, you can use your aura to better understand how to receive and work with this energy in your life.

Visualize the Perfect Job ·········

Many of us are taught that being employed means being unhappy and that repressing your wants and self-growth is a part of earning a living. However, understanding how your auric energy plays into your career choice proves this doesn't have to be the case. Visualizing your perfect day in a job you love can help you flip that programmed perception into one that inspires you. Perhaps as a red aura, being micromanaged by a boss is soul-crushing. Maybe as an indigo aura, you understand that working around people is too difficult and that your perfect day would be spent in a home office. Instead of limiting yourself based on what society says a job "should" be, use this activity to embark on a path to generate happiness.

TAKING ACTION

1. Enter a calm and relaxed state somewhere you will not be distracted. Take a few deep breaths, calming your mind as you do.
2. Ask yourself what a perfect day at work would be and visualize it: What would your work environment look like? What would the hours be? What does the hierarchy (if any) of upper management provide for you? Be specific in your responses.
3. Consider what your purpose in this work environment would be. What do you feel in this ideal environment?
4. Identify how your answers align with your aura. What does this visualization say about the authentic you?
5. When you close this visualization, take a mental note of what you felt and saw. When job hunting, use those feelings as a guide in the choices you make and the opportunities you seek out.

The things you like to do create realities around you—meaning, the better you like to do something, the better you do it.

Dissect Your Buyer's Remorse · · · · · · · · ·

Understanding why you felt annoyed, angry, or ashamed of yourself for purchasing something can provide feedback about your definition of self-worth. Different aura colors struggle with this in unique ways. The indigo aura who buys something they wanted for a long time yet didn't feel worthy of having may think they are undeserving of this item. The turquoise aura who bought an expensive gift to please a friend may feel incredible self-betrayal after realizing that they could not afford this gift. Buyer's remorse gives perspective into the ways your aura shows up when you aren't as aware of it as you need to be.

TAKING ACTION

1. Think of a purchase that was a clear case of buyer's remorse. What was the item? What in your mindset at the time prompted you to make that purchase?
2. Think about the moment you realized this was an unnecessary purchase. What is your reasoning for this realization?
3. Consider how your aura played into this purchase and how you feel it is reflected in your later remorse.
4. Ask yourself if it's necessary to still feel this way. Why or why not?

Understanding what it is about the regrets you have after a purchase will spotlight inner thoughts of your self-worth, impulses, and other moments you can reflect on to gain more control over your relationship with money and value.

Follow the Dollar ·········

One easy way to find out more about your relationship with money is by taking a look at it through the lens of your aura. Do you find a coffee habit creating havoc on your budget as a purple aura, or are you a pink aura with a monthly subscription to a shoe company that isn't exactly necessary? This activity is going to reveal what your energy is lacking, what value you are trying to create through spending, and what your energy could be communicating to you.

TAKING ACTION

1. Looking at your latest bank transaction history, think of a few words that sum up your spending and saving patterns. Would you say you are conservative to a fault? Perhaps prone to buying binges?

2. Ask yourself these questions: "What am I doing consistently?" "Why do I purchase this?" "What do I feel when I receive it?"

3. Reflect upon how your answers align with your aura, and in what ways your actions are creating unnecessary chaos.

4. Think about the value these patterned purchases are bringing to your life—if any. Take time to understand why or why not and brainstorm other ways you can invite the energy you seek. Perhaps that daily coffee trip could be replaced with a homemade brew and a walk. Or that impulse purchase could be substituted with a spontaneous meetup with a friend.

The little odds and ends in your money history are showing you things you look for, things you need, and holes in your life you want to fill. Your energy wants to be heard, and it finds interesting ways to make you listen. Follow the money to do just that.

Write Yourself a Check ·········

You were born to carry out your life's purpose. Money often seems like the point of it all, but what it really represents are opportunities for aura alignment. Feeling financially supported can bring clarity about which direction to go in. As a purple aura, if you didn't have to worry about money, you might travel to Italy for that art internship you desire. As a yellow aura, if you weren't so worried about paying bills, you could set up the social media marketing company you dream of. Thinking about what you want without the limitations of money can get your energy flowing.

TAKING ACTION

1. Write yourself a check, address it to yourself, and display it where you will see it often. In the "amount" line, put something that feels attainable to you. Writing "limitless abundance" also works.
2. Whenever you look at the check, repeat the mantra "I am financially abundant, and my dreams are plentiful." Do this as many times as it takes to say it confidently.
3. Ask yourself what you can do now that you have limitless funds. What have you been holding back on dreaming of because of money?
4. Consider how your dreams relate to your aura.

Giving yourself a free space for thinking without the constraints of money allows your aura to breathe, create, and be itself. It can thus begin to attract the opportunities that bring financial abundance and your wildest dreams.

CHAPTER 9

• • • • • • • • • • • •

Auras and
Personal Style

Whether you show it off through makeup, fashion, or decor, your personal style is a statement of your energy. Representing your aura through clothing and accessories or keeping it a focus when considering decorations and colors for spaces in your home can help you embrace your authentic vibe and create cohesion with your motivations, goals, and dreams. Your style creates a vibrational frequency around you that also interacts with other people. Subconsciously, they begin to better understand you as they pick up your carefully curated energy signature. They immediately form thoughts about you and attachments to you—all of which you have control over. There is power in choosing how your personal style reflects your authentic energy. The confidence you need or the emphasis on your intentions can all be promoted by your personal style. In your home, you can work with your aura to create the spaces your energy needs to feel safe and inspired to grow. In this chapter, you will create more cohesive connections between your style and the energy it encourages. Auras are often in the details, and a mindful awareness of how you present your energy aesthetically can also clue you in to how to take more control over your aura as you move forward.

What Your Aura Says about You

Each aura considers their personal style in a unique way.

····· RED ·····

A red aura's personal style is an assistant to their powerful vibration and reflects their need to be in control. Red auras have influential energies that present themselves in bold wardrobe selections. They often prefer luxury pieces and quality items over passing trends, as going with the whims of a fad is against their nature. They don't mind wearing vibrant colors in both their intimate surroundings and public settings to assist them in their ability to stand out and take charge. Red auras often prefer a modern yet classic vibe to their style, as they like forward-thinking fashion—reflective of their ability to change with the times while maintaining a sense of stability and decorum. Red auras crave focus and will pull elements into their personal style to redirect attention to where they are comfortable receiving it, such as a personal business logo, an extravagant watch, or a designer black pump. They tend to create workspaces that reflect their assertive style to calm and center them. Choosing large pieces that are enduring and impressive serves as a reminder to be worthy of the decor they have picked. Manifesting an air of influence in their overall energy signature, a red aura's personal style is about creating a dominant vibe while eliciting confidence from all those who enter into their auric atmosphere.

····· BLUE ·····

A blue aura cannot separate sentiment from anything they do, personal style being no exception. Therefore, blue auras often project their emotions and feelings upon items in their wardrobe and the rooms they spend most of their time in. Personification of their personal style can make it difficult to clear out closets and redo rooms, so blue auras often have consistent style patterns for much of their lifetimes. The sentiment they place in their wardrobe, accessories, and decor has value far above monetary worth. Blue auras prefer wearing clothing they attach fond memories to and heirloom pieces that bring them comfort, and creating rooms that are abundant in backstories and rich heritage. The purpose is to honor their story and create a space for it to be seen and enjoyed. Blue auras dislike standing out, so when wearing makeup, they tend to go with neutral basics and choose softer tones and hues for their clothes. Because blue auras are compassionate helpers, they often want style to follow function, preferring comfortable clothing that enables them to be of assistance to others. Blue auras rarely purchase anything for themselves, instead finding it more enjoyable to showcase antique or repurposed pieces in their homes and wear gifted accessories from those they love so dearly.

····· YELLOW ·····

Yellow auras are aware that their personal style is an accompaniment to their lifestyle. Therefore, they create polished worlds around them that not only reflect their taste but also can assist with their goals and dreams. Style speaks, and for a yellow aura, it articulates the structure they so crave in life via streamlined looks and timeless classic designs. Yellow auras are hardworking people, and the items they place on and around them reflect that. They enjoy well-made pieces that show careful workmanship and last for generations. The items they buy must be multipurpose to be worth the splurge, so they often justify bigger purchases with a running logic on the many ways the items will be utilized over the years. Yellow auras are always on the cusp of what's fashionable, but they will hold back to maintain their unique look. They can pair an amusing new fad subtly with a more time-honored design to suggest being on trend in a signature way. Yellow auras have a busy mind filled with ideas and to-do lists, yet they dislike clutter in life. The rooms in their homes are representative of their mindsets; when a yellow aura feels competent, their house reflects this, and they prioritize organizational systems to keep it so. They know that a structured environment can create flow for ideas, present a unified vibe, and create a secure state of self-confidence.

····· PURPLE ·····

Purple auras create their own style based on their current mood, oftentimes combining what they find inspirational with what they find comfortable. Purples enjoy evoking emotion in their wardrobe, both from themselves and others. Because purples love to spark change, anything that creates a reaction can be interesting to them. They don't shy away from moody vibes, shock value, or artistic expression with their style choices. While they can be aware of trends, they will choose an eclectic blend of modern with vintage to present their signature look to the world. Their style is full of vibrancy, and their decor will reflect that. Collections of mugs in the kitchen and random pops of color on the walls are signature purple aura interior designs. In all areas of their life, purple auras tend to move quickly and worry less about what's left in their wake, so their clothing and decor need to be good with tough wear and use. You won't find them wearing dry-clean-only fabrics, as anything that requires maintenance won't receive it from the purple aura. They often lose or damage their pieces, so they choose accessories that aren't very valuable. The purple aura style is about change, so their style choices are symbolic of the quirky, creative, and sometimes messy way they prefer to live life.

····· GREEN ·····

Green auras have a practical view of life, and their style often reflects it. Because green auras are more about practicality than traditional ideas of fashion, they end up choosing a timeless style and sticking to it. They have no problem wearing the same type of clothing for years to come if it works for them and makes them feel comfortable. Attention to passing whims of fashion isn't within the green aura's bandwidth. They do love quality with their style, choosing long-lasting and well-sourced pieces for their collection. A well-made watch, a handcrafted chair, or a durable winter coat are easy choices for a green aura who knows they will be used for many years to come. The home of a green aura reflects their needs, current projects, and what they consider to be utilitarian. A fully stocked garden house or a basement with a complete set of tools is a green aura's idea of a well-designed home. Green auras don't mind spending extra on anything that lasts. They are very concerned with the origins of what they wear, as well as craftsmanship and their own personal responsibility as a consumer. Green auras are aware of the global implications about what materials are used to create a piece of furniture or clothing they wear and will happily upcycle and research brands carefully.

· · · · · INDIGO · · · · ·

To be comfortably invisible is the indigo aura's fashion goal. While they are careful not to stand out too much via loud colors or edgy fashion trends, they do care a lot for quality items. Indigo auras will splurge on anything that is cozy, tailored, and has a sense of character that feels charming to them. They research brands carefully and love to incorporate stories into their purchases. A handmade sweater by a small business or a handcrafted armchair made from a unique piece of reclaimed wood are examples of pieces the indigo aura considers to be extra-precious. An indigo aura's home is truly their safe space, and their decor will reflect that. Low lighting and pieces that encourage rest and reading are abundant. Indigos value sentiment and place much worth in their heirloom and meaningful pieces. They are often the keepers of multiple family relics, and finding ways to incorporate those items into their personal style is an expression of love for the indigo aura. Taking old wedding rings and molding them into necklace charms or making sure the family's latest bride is wearing a great-grandmother's hairpin are things the indigo aura takes much pride in. Indigo auras are a soft place to land in life for those who can see their quietly profound energetic signature.

· · · · · PINK · · · · ·

Pink auras are motivated to find their joy in their wardrobe. Pieces that reflect their latest fascination or remind them of days gone by are often found in the pink aura's style inventory. Pink auras often fixate on one trend at a time. With their wardrobe, decor, and accessories, they can create a means of escape from reality, so they do tend to become stuck in past fashion regardless of whether it's considered back in style or not. But the pink aura pays little attention to how others view them. Pink auras bring all the sense of wonder into their home decor as well, as they focus on whimsical lighting, fun looks, and unique spaces that inspire creative thought and escapist vibes. Re-creating a dream bedroom from their childhood or choosing unorthodox appliance colors is how pink auras bring out their inner child in interior design. Pink auras don't mind colors that pop, and they will even wear pieces most people find uncomfortable. Tight clothing, high-heeled shoes, and impractical earrings are all in the pink aura's style range. Pink auras send out a unique message to the world through their personal style, and the message is that their style is completely representative of what they want and not contingent on the thoughts of anyone else.

· · · · · TURQUOISE · · · · ·

Turquoise auras need flow in all they do, and their style is no exception. They love fabrics that move and have comfort and grace. A turquoise aura brings an atmosphere of possibility into their style, and they curate this energy with vibrant combinations of patterns and textures. They enjoy borrowing looks from many different aesthetics to create their unique style signature. It's not uncommon to see them pair embroidered bracelets with heirloom items, or upcycled thrift store pieces with a remnant of their grandparent's wardrobe. They are always construct-ing their style based upon current moods and passions. Turquoise auras treat their homes like havens, and they construct magical places to live in. Shelves filled with crystals and walls bright with paintings are found in the abodes of turquoise auras. They enjoy secondhand items and anything handmade and meaningful. The homes of turquoise auras can present a multitude of genres at once, as they go by their instinct rather than a need to adhere to any standard. Turquoise auras don't enjoy choosing just one way of being in anything they do.

· · · · · **ORANGE** · · · · ·

The style of an orange aura is about power—and how they can best communicate that power. Orange auras will never settle for anything less than best-dressed, and their style knows no budget when it comes to accomplishing this task. Orange auras like tailored pieces that bring focus to the parts of themselves they want to highlight. Strong lines in suits, shoes that demonstrate wealth, and accessories that are not subtle about their value are ostentatiously worn at all times. Orange auras are typically very self-aware of their own perceived physical flaws, which can hinder their ability to win the confidence they are looking for. Therefore, they spend a lot of time and budget on crafting looks that hide seeming imperfections. Lifted shoes, carefully constructed hair and makeup, and professional tailoring that gives the illusion of height or svelte physique are common items in the orange aura's wardrobe. Their homes are fur-ther contexts for them to promote their image. Fine finishings are valued over comfort, and orange auras are not shy about redecorating as often as needed. Staying up to date on trends both in home and fashion shows their ability to remain on the pulse of society.

embracing your aura

Confront the Closet ·········

Your closet says a lot about you and your energy. Blue auras may have a difficult time parting with a sweater that holds a wonderful memory but is no longer a viable fashion statement. Green auras may find themselves staring at a row of the same-style shirt in various shades. Going into your closet mindfully with an awareness of your aura will provide insight into what might no longer speak to who you authentically are, what you might want to purchase more of, and where you could be limiting yourself. It's time to confront your closet.

TAKING ACTION

1. Before entering your closet, ask yourself what you feel your aura says about you that you want others to notice.
2. Now ask yourself what parts of your aura you would like your style to enhance and support. And what *don't* you want to convey with your wardrobe?
3. With this mindset, enter your closet.
4. Organize your clothes and accessories into piles of what you will keep, what you can donate, and what you want to reevaluate now that you are focused on your authentic energy.

Confronting the closet can be a daunting task for a very good reason: Your energy is attached to the things you have. When you let go of what doesn't work for you anymore with your energy in mind, you open up more space for your unique self to shine.

Reacquaint Yourself with an Old Favorite · · · · · · · ·

The clothing we choose to wear every day says a lot about our energy signatures. It introduces us to the world before we do—in fact, it's a bit of a calling card. There are pieces in your closet that are without a doubt quintessentially you. Perhaps it's the old concert T-shirt that makes your purple aura ignite upon sight or a pair of classic shoes that your yellow aura finds timeless. Finding a favorite piece of clothing in your wardrobe is like finding a bit of yourself. These pieces are complete reflections of your authentic aura, and honoring them is very much honoring you.

TAKING ACTION

1. Go into your closet and find something that simply makes you smile.
2. Take a careful look at your selection. Sit with it for a while and reflect on what makes it a favorite of yours.
3. Ask yourself what it is about this piece that reflects your aura colors, and how it does so.
4. Keep in mind what this piece means to you and how it makes you feel when you are shopping for new items to add to your wardrobe.

The little pieces of your energy that get tucked away in special spots like this are precious. They often contain bits you may have forgotten about or thought you put away for good. Bring them out and show them off again!

Create a New Outfit to Showcase Your Aura · · · · · · · ·

In everyday life, there is usually a rush to get dressed and ready. Oftentimes, you may mindlessly choose looks that either feel comfortable or help you to blend in with the crowd. However, as you look back, you probably can remember certain styles and outfits that made you feel very special, very comfortable, and very much yourself. These were looks that reflected your aura. Whether it's pairing a thrift store favorite with some new pieces as a turquoise aura or giving some power boardroom vibes in a sharp suit as an orange aura, an outfit can really showcase your vibe.

TAKING ACTION

1. Think about a time in your life you really felt like yourself in an outfit. What were you wearing? How exactly did it make you feel?
2. Consider how your answers in step one relate to your aura colors.
3. Using either your current wardrobe or recent purchases, create a new look by referencing the aura guide earlier in this chapter to identify pieces that best align with your aura.
4. Wear your outfit out! Take note of how you feel.

When your style can speak for you, when it assists in communicating who you are to others, you can feel very content, confident, and joyful. It's not about what others think; it's about how you are connecting to something deeper within yourself.

Take an Accessory Inventory ·········

Those little added touches to your wardrobe aren't just fun or stylish; they can assist you in expressing your aura. They are an accompaniment to your existing vibe, motivations, goals, and dreams. As you look at your accessory collection, you will be reflecting on how your aura shows up in your selections. Perhaps it's an array of past and present trending pieces, such as a purple aura may have, or an organized selection of timeless treasures a yellow aura may show off. The way you keep your collection and how you have chosen your pieces say a lot about your aura.

TAKING ACTION

1. Review and record your current collection of accessories.
2. Create an overall impression of your collection. Notice the patterns of styles, colors, and history of pieces. As you do so, ask yourself what the collection says about your aura colors.
3. If you find you don't have much of a collection to review, or if it doesn't seem to follow a pattern at all, create a list of what accessories you feel you could add to reflect your personal auric style.

The pieces you accessorize with can say a lot about you to those you come into contact with. They tell an energetic story. The pieces collected throughout your lifetime can show off who you are and make a statement to the world that can be very personal and specific.

Accessorize for the Occasion ·········

Different occasions elicit different emotions, and these particular emotions reflect your energetic signature. What you want to say energetically in a certain setting—and how you want to say it—can be expressed quite loudly through your accessories. A blue aura may choose an heirloom necklace for comfort during a special occasion, whereas a red aura may go for a designer watch to convey their powerful presence in a business meeting. It's time to dig a little deeper into what you wear to different events and why.

TAKING ACTION

1. Ask yourself what you would wear to a few different events or occasions, such as a wedding, an interview, or a night out with friends.
2. Reflect on what each of these occasions brings up for you emotionally and how these reactions reflect your aura colors.
3. Think about the accessories you wear when you want to project a certain vibe, like when you need to feel brave, when you are going somewhere special and want to be noticed, or when you want to be cozy and connect with the people around you.
4. Ask yourself how each of your accessory options assists and supports the emotions you identified in step two.
5. Use your answers to start accessorizing based on the feeling you are pursuing.

Accessories offer a simple but limitless way to express your energy and capture the feeling of an occasion.

Add a Pop of Aura Color ·········

Auras are cozily hidden away in the details of our most sacred spaces: our homes. Adding a pop of color to a room is more than just a way to contribute to your decor; it amplifies who you are and acts as a reminder to take yourself into consideration in your space. Perhaps your kitchen needs some bright greenery brought in from the outside to make your green aura feel at peace, or maybe your bedroom could use a new indigo bedspread to remind your indigo aura to settle in and sleep easily in your safe space. Thoughtfully placing your aura colors in places where you spend a lot of quality time is a simple way to celebrate yourself.

TAKING ACTION

1. Take an inventory of your home, and choose a room or a section of a space that you feel the most need to bring more of your energy into.
2. Reflect on what this space is naturally used for and how you can flow with that use while adding in your aura color.
3. Bring in a pop of you in aura color, be it in an item or a paint color that reflects who you are energetically.

Respecting the space that nurtures your energy is validating. It allows your energy to feel safe and grow and provides a healthy atmosphere for both your physical and spiritual bodies.

Borrow a Vibe ·········

Colors reflect moods and tones, and their link to energy is something you can use to shape the purpose of the space you are in. Perhaps your purple aura needs focus with a green accent wall in your office, or maybe your bathroom could use a blue vase to remind your yellow aura to calm down and center. Borrowing a vibe through color in a room or smaller space meant for something specific is a simple way to claim your energy and work with its unique strengths and weaknesses.

TAKING ACTION

1. Choose a room or space that has a specific purpose and reflect upon what exactly that purpose is.
2. Reflect mindfully upon what you need to do here versus what this room is actually used for.
3. Ask yourself what you could use more of energetically in this room—something you struggle with when trying to use this space effectively.
4. Grab some paint or other artistic touch that reflects a vibe you want to borrow for this space and add it wherever you like.

While living authentically is the goal, you sometimes need to support your existing energies with some complementary vibes you do not own. Borrowing a vibe to assist your aura in tasks you find difficult can provide more structure and motivation to certain spaces in your home. Now you can take what you need and leave the rest.

Make a Room for YOU ·········

It's time to rethink how you spend your most precious energy in the rooms and spaces of where you live. Your home is a haven for you to be your most authentic self, to recharge and to get ready to face the world again. Many times, you end up focusing on your spaces' typical functions, which are necessary but are not always a reflection of who you are or how you authentically do things. You can forget to make the space for the things that feed your aura and bring you joy. Perhaps it's as simple as a reading nook that warms your blue aura heart or a corner for fitness activities that gets your red aura inspired. For this activity, you will choose a room or smaller space in your home that you can revamp to completely reflect your auric signature.

TAKING ACTION

1. Choose a space to redecorate.
2. Brainstorm the limitless possibilities of what you would like to have in this space that is totally and completely about you.
3. Take a step back and look around your space. Ask yourself what things you can do within budget and reason to bring in some of the elements of your brainstorming activity.
4. Rearrange the space to reflect you.

Little changes that align with your inherent auric energy can make a huge difference. Mindfully choosing pieces and colors that support your unique vibration allows you to function more freely in the place that is supposed to nurture you most.

CHAPTER 10

. . . .

Auras and Creativity and Fun

There is a programmed belief in society—one that tells you to put away who you really are for what you "should" be doing instead. The need to be accepted becomes silently linked to your very survival. You may fear the consequences of stepping outside of what others find "correct," being judged or unsafe, or having to confront a life built upon who you thought you were and not who you actually are. But your energy yearns to flow outwardly and leave its unique mark upon the world. It begs you to allow it to do so, and you feel it doing so in your dreams, wayward thoughts, and moments of clarity that slice their way through to your conscious mind. Your aura glows radiantly when you embrace the things, places, and people that encourage it to truly flourish. You don't have to make a huge leap: Even the tiniest steps are powerful. Understanding your likes, creative pursuits, and spaces where you find joy is a simple path toward embracing more of yourself and your aura. In this chapter, you will reawaken your creative flow and joy to not just live life in a more aurically aligned way, but to also have fun while doing so.

What Your Aura Says about You

Each aura approaches creativity and fun in unique ways.

····· RED ·····

Red auras look for legacy in all that they do: a way to generationally pass down the energy they so valiantly give to those around them. Their creative endeavors support this need to be remembered and honored, and because of this, creating a name for themselves becomes their preferred life purpose. Red auras enjoy the feeling that what they have done matters, and they spend a lot of time and energy thinking of ways to carry on the benefits of who they are in a way that will impact others for years to come. A plot of land that hosts their family for generations or a change within society accredited to their hard work and vision are creative outlets that red auras pursue. The need to make sure they left this space better than how they found it is where they invest their creativity. Red auras don't mind a little credit; in fact, they like to be the reason others have their own inspired ideas to leave meaningful legacies. Red auras love to feel the united energy of people coming together to complete a common goal. Joining forces to rally on a favorite team, gathering together to build houses for those in need, or getting old friends together to lift up a friend in need are all in the red aura's wheelhouse of fun.

····· BLUE ·····

The blue aura often encounters their creative voice among their pursuits of helping others. They enjoy new ways of seeing people and develop new methods to express this ability to do so. Their knack for seeing what is needed and finding ways to express their unique voice while doing it is a valuable multitasking skill that blue auras master. Creating the perfect cake for the birthday boy they adore, organizing the secret retirement party for the coworker they love, or making a friend feel extra-special by scrapbooking their memorable year together is how their true self emerges. Blue auras don't skimp on making sure someone knows they've seen them—the real them. They know what it is to feel a bit tucked away energetically, so they find joy in their ability to allow others to feel seen and loved. Blue auras have fun seeing others relax and share that energy in social and intimate gatherings alike. A child's birthday party, a movie night in with close friends, or a day spent supporting a local charity are all ways blue auras have a wonderful time. Being authentically in their own beautiful need to compassionately give and validate the emotions of others is how blue auras can find some fun in the everyday. Seeing how they can put their own creative spin on what they find closes the loop on what giving to others gives back to them.

· · · · · YELLOW · · · · ·

Finding the scaffolding needed to build great things is a yellow aura's specialty, and the way they do this is how they express their unique perspective to the world. Yellow auras can see the bigger picture and break it down into manageable parts. In this way, they can infuse the vision with their own energy, allowing for their individual voice to be heard and experienced. Yellow auras are creative in ways others notice immediately, for they merge their innovation with improving life in some way. Yellow auras are also visual people, so their artistic expression comes in delights of the senses. The thoughtfulness of the yellow aura's creativity is what makes it so unique and appreciated. The perfect wallpaper to match your eyes in the room they redecorated just for you, the charcuterie table with all your favorite things laid out at a get-together, or a special memory moment crafted at the event they planned in your honor are all outlets for yellow aura creativity. They are attracted to photography, event planning, and interior design. Self-improvement and new ways to unlock their potential give yellow auras that burst of endorphins that make life even more enjoyable. Taking a spiritual workshop, learning a new language, or getting the self-help audiobook they've heard so much about isn't tedious to them: It's fun!

· · · · · PURPLE · · · · ·

The freedom of self-expression is one that purple auras fight for in all aspects of their life. Oppression can come in many forms in their world, the celebrated societal structure being the main one, and the little victories they claim in the battle to rebel are proudly enjoyed. Purple auras need to make space in their mindset to explore themselves so they can create freedom on all energetic planes. Getting lost in a drawing, dancing to a well-curated playlist, or spending carefree times with close friends are all necessary contexts for doing this. The idea that doing what they love in life isn't a way to make a living is harmful to the purple aura. The spirit of rebellion is the purple aura's greatest creative tool, and when this is used in a mindful way, they can do what they love—and make a living. Open mic night becomes a full-time gig, a penchant for graphic design becomes a livable income, and an ability to talk to anyone creates the networking skills needed to have the perfect job with the flex schedule. Purple auras find that creativity is the way to survive, and their ability to see beyond what many can is how they do that. Promoting a bit of rebellion in the places it feels forbidden is a purple aura's specialty. Purple auras don't like society to tell them what to do, and pushing those lines while redrawing their own is how they have a good time.

· · · · · GREEN · · · · ·

The green aura finds their creative voice by building bridges between two spaces without requiring communication to do so. They have the ability to envision something that could work that isn't in existence—in what ways they can build a stronger and more effective synergy between unlike spaces. Green auras need challenge, and when embarking upon a new project, they themselves become reworked and more efficient in the process. Through these methods, their creativity expresses itself as ingenuity—an inventive spirit that manifests what is needed. The rebuilding of antique cars, finding new ways to fertilize their garden, or pitching an innovative approach to running a Fortune 500 company are all ways in which the green aura expresses their creativity. No matter which context the green aura chooses to show off their authentic self, the way they can create a world around it completely of their own design is what is to be admired. The green aura comprehends that to be completely and joyfully creative, they must find ways to achieve that state that others may not understand. Green auras delight in learning challenging yet impressive skills, such as how to take professional-grade photos, rock climbing, or restoring antique furniture to its original glory. Teaching others how to enjoy what they do brings a new level of entertainment to the green aura, one that streamlines their own happiness straight to the energy of another.

····· INDIGO ·····

In their quest to separate their interests from the ones they constantly serve, indigo auras seek out creativity in quiet spots. In peaceful moments, they can finally feel their creative voice emerge, and as they do so, the analytic tendencies it often takes on become vibrant and loud. Indigo auras find their fun in categorizing the world and reflecting on what makes people act as they do—which parts of the unhealed self affect conscious or subconscious actions. The pursuit of ways to communicate this is fascinating to the indigo aura, and they enjoy the multitude of possibilities for expressing their findings. Through creative writing, journaling, and sometimes painting or crafting, they find innovative new connections and send out this insight so that others may see what they see. The indigo aura learns that their perspective is a unique one; therefore, their findings are best expressed in ways others can clearly receive them. As they foster creative flow between their insights and how to deliver them, they find bits of themselves along the way. The unearthing of truths and gems of insight is the indigo aura's reward for their creative efforts.

· · · · · PINK · · · · ·

Making magic isn't something most people can claim to excel at, but pink auras do this in every aspect of their lives. Creating isn't just about aesthetic decor or a fashionable outfit; it's about an air of allure. Pinks create an enigma of a personality—a playful mystery that everyone turns their heads toward. Pink auras create possibility; in a world that likes to snuff the flame of individuality, they double down on their own. They don't just create with their material world; they create with the very universe that seems to rotate around their energetic self. Pink auras love the feeling of delight, and they use their artistic voices to find new ways to foster this feeling, not just for them but also for whoever wishes to enter their energetic domain. A whimsical party, a quintessential sleepover, or a room that seems to be straight out of one's childhood dreams is what pink auras spend their creative efforts on. Their purpose *seems* to be some sort of escapism, but in reality, it is about creating a place where one can truly feel unlimited by the laws governing society. They allow others to enter the wonderland that they thought had expired long ago in a childhood memory.

· · · · · TURQUOISE · · · · ·

Living on the fringe of everyone's energies gives the turquoise aura a unique perspective of our world. Turquoise auras understand what it is to be unseen and forgotten. Their ever-changing energy can be dispersed and saturated quite easily. Because of this, they are very sensitive to noticing the ways that people throw themselves away and what things in our world are forgotten about entirely. Turquoise auras love energy, and they express their creativity as they care for forgotten pieces of it. They find it inspiring to work with similarly discarded and misused energy they find out in the world among those they interact with. In this way, they end up using a lot of their artistic expression in playing with that energy and repurposing it. Finding unique items and creating art out of them, working with energy healing and crystals, or crafting unique jewelry that holds the energy they so dearly respect are ways that turquoise auras express themselves. It's not uncommon for a turquoise aura to find themselves as they care for a neglected garden or upcycle clothing. Turquoise auras give what has been forgotten a new voice and remind people of who they are and what they have lost. Turquoise auras have fun when they are feeling carefree around like-minded, nonjudgmental people.

· · · · · **ORANGE** · · · · ·

There are so many ways to express oneself, and the orange aura is on the hunt to uncover them all. Orange auras live to feel the freedom of self-expression, and they often end up articulating it well, branding it, and attaching a PR firm to promote it. Orange auras use their creative voice in business endeavors, political engagements, the entertainment industry, and in all ways they can showcase their ideas. They love to feel their freedom by watching their life affect others. What they say, they believe wholeheartedly, making them hard to ignore by the masses. The orange aura uses their energy as a creative force, plowing new paths in a society that would sometimes rather be left to a quiet routine. Orange auras aren't afraid of how they can change what they see simply by what they say. They accumulate influence so as to have that very effect. For them, change is creative energy in full expression; the upending skills they so inherently possess are their brushstrokes among humanity itself. Orange auras move up the ladder of influence to use this skill to its maximum degree, and they savor the phenomenon that occurs when others praise them for it.

Orange auras have fun when they are winning at life and things are going their way. They love being surrounded by people who are influenced and inspired by their often very forward and well-articulated ideas, and they relish every moment of the success they work so hard to achieve.

embracing your aura

Throw an Aura Party ·········

A great party is one where the guests can really experience the host's authentic self. The personalized touches, the fun little details, and the overall vibe that clearly reflects the host's enthusiasm make all the difference. Perhaps it's the red aura's favorite barbecue treats served for dinner or the pink aura's candy station set up in the corner. Guests don't want to always experience what they already know they like—they enjoy seeing your ideas and tastes come to life too. Throwing a party that reflects who you are by leaning into your aura allows you to celebrate your creative self *and* extend your authentic frequency to all who attend. It provides not just a fun time for everyone but also one where you feel totally yourself.

TAKING ACTION

1. Think about what your ideal party would include. Don't focus so much on what you think a party "should" have based on others you've attended. Rather, consider what speaks specifically to your ideas of fun.
2. Get planning: Pick a date, buy any items you need, send out the invites, and enlist friends' help if you need it.
3. Enjoy the party!
4. After the party, reflect on feedback received from guests, your own emotions, and how it all relates to your aura.

When you showcase what "fun" looks like to you, and include others in it, you can extend your good time to people who will appreciate it.

Find Fun in the Mundane ·········

Life doesn't always afford us the time we need to feel as creative as we could or to have fun when we want to. Work, responsibilities, and daily challenges can impede our fantasies of exploring an interest we've long had or cancel a fun outing due to constraints on funds and time. However, finding the fun in the mundane will allow you to explore your creativity and find pleasure no matter what life's circumstances may throw your way. The turquoise aura who finds joy upcycling and swapping their child's clothing with friends makes a necessary chore a fun and creative get-together. The purple aura who drives their car all day for their job creates unique and creative playlists to listen to while doing so. Finding your fun in a seemingly mundane routine uncovers and strengthens your self-connection.

TAKING ACTION

1. Think about tasks you have in life that are mundane.
2. Reflect upon how you could make these tasks more fun and creative based on your aura colors.
3. Complete one of these tasks with this new intention of finding fun where you can in it. Note how you feel during and after the task.

Finding the small ways you can turn a seemingly mundane task into a means of creative expression makes life a little less dull and a lot more fun.

Introduce Yourself with Your Unique Brand of Creativity ········

Long gone are the days you were asked to introduce yourself to others in a classroom situation. Little children are given paper and crayons, and without a second thought, they are encouraged to write all about who they are, celebrating the differences as they read them aloud. As we get older, the parts of us that are unique are instead criticized, called out, and made to feel awkward instead of special. Our creative selves get shelved in order to fit in and complete tasks in a more standardized and unoriginal way. Reclaiming who you are with the ease of when you were small is a wonderful activity for reigniting your creative aura.

TAKING ACTION

1. Take a blank sheet of paper and introduce yourself with no inhibitions. Draw or write that which makes you, you. Tap into your inner child for guidance on having fun and forgetting what you think you "should" say and how you "should" say it.
2. As you create your introduction, ask yourself how what you are saying relates to your aura.
3. Reflect on how you think your introduction differed as a child. How do you think your creative self still shows itself today?
4. Hang this creation proudly where you can see it and delight in your aura regularly.

Whatever difficulty you met while completing this activity will relate to how in touch you are with your creative aura. Meeting your aura in this genuine and innocent way can have a profound effect on how you pursue creativity and fun moving forward.

Leave Your Creative Comfort Zone ·········

Making yourself go far outside your comfort zone does something really interesting to your energy: In your discomfort, it actually blasts away existing creative blockages that come with doing things the same way for far too long. The red aura who is dragged to the Reiki healing finds new ways to create energetic control. The yellow aura who decides to join the hip-hop class unleashes pent-up anxiety by doing something completely and utterly imperfect in front of a bunch of people. They can then transfer this bravery to new creative contexts. It's time to get uncomfortable in order to remove blockages that have been stifling your creative energy.

TAKING ACTION

1. Enlist a friend or make your own plan to do something completely out of your comfort zone. For example, take an acting class, sign up for surfing lessons, or commit to learning a new language.
2. Embrace the awkward as you embark upon this activity.
3. Notice your feelings during it. Reflect upon naming them and giving a voice to them.
4. How do these emotions you experience tell you about your auric energy?

When taken out of your routine and put in a place where you can't use habits to blend in, you are forced instead to get a little inventive. Thinking of ways you can embrace these newfound skills in the future can assist you on your journey to evolving your creative self.

"Aura-Splain" Your Interest · · · · · · · · ·

The things you enjoy the most are creative expressions of your aura. The consistent fitness regimen the red aura enjoys or the love of party planning the pink aura may exhibit are examples of true auric expression. It could be a small thing you love, such as cuddling up with your favorite book series, as a blue aura might, or tending to a neighbor's dying hedge, as a green aura is likely to do. Explaining your favorite interests through the lens of your aura colors is a way for you to not only connect with yourself but also make more choices in your life that promote fun and creativity.

TAKING ACTION

1. Reflect upon an activity that you love.
2. Consider your emotional state before this activity.
3. Do the activity, and be mindful of how your emotions shift as you do.
4. Reflect on your emotional state after finishing the activity.
5. Think about how this activity and the ways it impacted your emotions connect to your aura.
6. Brainstorm ways you can bring this activity into other areas of your life, such as volunteering to plan work events, as a pink aura might, or starting a book club, as a blue aura might.

The things you love the most aren't wastes of time; rather, they are places in which you can meet your uniquely creative self. Embracing your motivation as an expression of your aura will allow you to foster more opportunities to be yourself—and have fun doing it.

Take Your Creative Inventory · · · · · · · ·

You may be missing opportunities to get more creative. Life is busy, and being in a numb, detached state can at times feel easier than stretching yourself to live in a more creative vibration. Stating goals to get more creative can assist you with living your true aura colors out loud. Putting them into action gives you that needed boost into a leveled-up auric experience. You can finally take a virtual class on how to macramé, as a turquoise aura may have been meaning to do, or decide to create that business logo for your Etsy shop, as the yellow aura has been procrastinating on for some time now. The tiniest creative goals set your aura colors ablaze!

TAKING ACTION

1. Thinking about your aura colors, what do you feel you are missing out on that you want to create more of?
2. Make a mental note of one to three creative goals based on what you come up with in step one.
3. Visualize what life would be like if these goals were met. How would these goals—and life as a whole—align with your authentic energy?

Prioritizing your creativity in life is essential to evolving energetically. Your aura needs to move and play, just like your physical body does, to stay healthy, aligned, and working for you. Make some new creativity goals every few months to enjoy the full benefits of your aura.

Do Daily Moments · · · · · · · · ·

Doing a little bit for yourself every day creates more than a little bit of change; it can turn your life in a whole new direction. Breaking down your creative goals into smaller parts is how you make this shift, like the red aura who decides to take back their life by emailing a few business prospects every day during their lunch break, or the green aura who spends a few moments sketching out the plans for their new invention each evening. Taking on the big goal and inching toward it in some way every day is what creates communication between your authentic energy and the ways it can be expressed.

TAKING ACTION

1. Think of a creative goal you want to achieve.
2. Brainstorm one small thing you can do in the spirit of this goal today, then do it.
3. Afterward, connect with your feelings. Does this step make you feel inspired? Overwhelmed?
4. Continue setting smaller goals each day leading up to the achievement of your larger dream. For example, the red aura levels up their steps by scheduling interviews. The green aura takes those completed blueprints to a patent lawyer for review.

Defining what you want in life can be very overwhelming, but taking tiny steps toward your goal makes it doable. Prioritizing time during your day creates an energy around you of healthy auric growth. The more you can give to this vibration, the more the world will create opportunities and inspiration to get you to where you eventually want to be.

Get Creative with Others ·········

The ways you showcase your creative self are unique and grounded firmly in your auric energy. You can gain confidence in your own creative abilities when you begin to show them off proudly for others to see and experience. A pink aura may decide to take on the task of planning an ice cream party for their coworkers; a yellow aura may decide to bring their label maker over to organize a friend's pantry. Getting creative with others is going to showcase your aura in a way that brings you confidence and clarity about how you bring value to the world around you.

TAKING ACTION

1. Gather some ideas for where your creative talents could be put to good use and enjoyed with a friend, family member, etc. Think about what's fun for you to do!
2. Make a plan to do one of these things with someone.
3. After having a little creative fun, reflect upon the aura colors of the other person and yourself. In what ways did your creativity assist them? In what ways did their creativity contribute to the activity?

Being present enough to really consider how your unique creative energy is a complement to others gives you a new perspective on your inherent gifts. Additionally, you can find inspiration for new creative pursuits through the talents of others.

Cleansing Your Aura

Why Cleanse Your Aura?

When your aura is at its healthiest, you become more in tune psychically with the world around you, since your aura, when in a cleansed state, is like a beacon for messages from the divine and your own intuition. A healthy aura is also able to sense danger, see through lies others tell you, assist you in seeing a person's true motives and intentions, and connect with others through astral travel. Additionally, when your aura is cleansed regularly, your physical health improves. You can heal yourself more easily and create boundaries with increased "psychic armor" (the ability to shut out negative energies). Most importantly, you make better choices for yourself because you can make distinctions between your authentic self and the needs, emotions, and wants of others. You can choose between what you want to do and what others want from you, allowing you to make the choices and creative advances that bring your life joy and purpose.

You can picture your aura much like a cozy sweater wrapped around you all the time. Just like a sweater, it can collect the lint and fibers of the environments it encounters throughout the day. Every once in a while, you need to run a lint roller over the sweater to rid it of what it has collected. Your aura collects energies from the environments you enter, the media you consume, the people you interact with, and the past traumas you've held on to. These are the things that need to be cleansed to keep your aura at its healthiest. Taking the time to cleanse your aura can be difficult when life consistently presents you with things you feel you have to do instead. However, much like your daily habits of showering and brushing your teeth, cleaning your aura is an act of self-care that must not be skipped. Make a persistent and consistent effort to work it into your routine. In time, you'll be able to recognize when you need a cleanse.

Aura Cleansing Techniques

Cleansing your aura can provide you with clarity and calmness. Try out the following simple techniques to determine which works best for you.

DO PROTECTION MEDITATIONS

Regularly envisioning your aura as a bubble of protection around you is key to keeping it maintained and functioning properly. Just like any muscle, your aura becomes stronger when you focus on it daily and work on it with intention. Use these steps to complete a protection meditation:

1. While lying down, visualize the white light of Spirit entering into your third eye (the space between your eyebrows) and filling you with positive and healing energy.
2. Feel this light expel any negativity within you, forming a bubble of protection all around your body.
3. In your mind's eye, see the colors of your aura that make up this bubble.
4. Using your third eye vision, look all around this bubble for any rips within the auric shield.
5. If you see any rips, just send more healing light to these spots, and know they will be repaired.

6. When you feel that your bubble looks strong and feels complete, exit your meditative state. Say the words "I am protected," and know this bubble of auric protection travels with you all the time, working for you as you go about your daily life.

STAY TRUE TO WHO YOU ARE

Your aura feeds off authenticity. When you rush to say yes to something you really don't want to do, your aura suffers. When you force yourself to go to a place every day that doesn't align with your goals and mental health, your aura weakens. It needs to be validated and heard, and every thought, word, and action needs to reflect who you are inside. Keeping a journal where you write how you feel without judgment is helpful. Being truthful to yourself instead of covering up your real feelings to fit in is essential to the health of your aura.

BATHE

On a really bad day, there's nothing like a restorative bath. The healing properties of water are unmatched and can cleanse your aura in an enjoyable way. Follow these steps to rejuvenate your energy with a bath:

1. Draw a bath to your preferred temperature and add Epsom salt to your liking.
2. Light a candle and set up an essential oil diffuser if you have one.
3. Enter this bath with the intention of wiping away anything in your aura that is not yours, repairing any energy tears and repeating intentions that give a feeling of wholeness and protection.
4. Relax and focus on the visualization of your energy being repaired and cleansed as you bathe.
5. When you drain the bath, know that anything that does not serve you leaves with the water.

The grounding properties of water and salt will enlist the energy of the earth to cleanse your aura.

USE SOUND

Listening to binaural beats in alpha frequencies (8 to 13 Hz) can create a deeper level of meditation, promote your ability to connect to your aura, and reduce stress and anxiety. Regularly listening to them before sleep, when stressed, or whenever you feel the need will improve your ability to cleanse your aura. The state of being you create when listening to these frequencies is aligned with your Higher Self, a union that is powerful and authentic and, therefore, very peaceful and calming.

USE A CRYSTAL

If you enjoy working with crystals, you can choose a crystal and use it to cleanse your aura. Selenite (assists in connecting to higher realms), amethyst (creates serenity), or blue lace agate (supports confident communication) work really well. Follow these steps:

1. Place the crystal on your third eye (the space above your brow line between your eyes).
2. Repeat the mantra "I am cleansed, I am protected." As you do, feel the crystal aligning itself with your mantra and your energy.
3. When you feel the crystal has infused itself with your mantra and your energy, you may stop.
4. Keep the crystal in your pocket or purse as a touchstone for your aura protection when you feel nervous, upset, or untethered throughout your day.

index

about the author

Mystic Michaela (Megan Firester) is a fourth-generation psychic medium. Her true passion is guiding people through Spirit to live their own authentic lives. Michaela currently resides in South Florida, where she has a thriving practice of personal clients. She is also the host of her own podcast, *Know Your Aura with Mystic Michaela*. She has been featured as a New Age expert in *Well+Good*, *Cosmopolitan*, *Shape*, *Women's Health*, *Elle*, and more.